BEYOND THE POTTER'S HOUSE

BEYOND THE
POTTER'S HOUSE

THE CALL, THE CONSECRATION,
AND THE COMMISSION OF THE HOLY SPIRIT

THE PREACHER®

DESTINY IMAGE™ EUROPE srl
Via Maiella, 1
66020 San Giovanni Teatino (Ch) - Italy

"Changing the world, one book at a time."

This book and all other Destiny Image™ Europe books are available at Christian bookstores and distributors worldwide.

To order products, or for any other correspondence:

DESTINY IMAGE™ EUROPE srl
Via Acquacorrente, 6
65123 - Pescara - Italy
Tel. +39 085 4716623 - Fax +39 085 9431270
E-mail: info@eurodestinyimage.com

Or reach us on the Internet: **www.eurodestinyimage.com**

ISBN: 978-88-89127-87-2
For Worldwide Distribution, Printed in the U.S.A.
1 2 3 4 5 6 7 8/13 12 11 10 09

Acknowledgments

After Him whose breath inspires my pen, I wish to thank, for this volume, my brother, Pastor Pietro Evangelista, for his encouragement by e-mails and telephone calls—and what a debt I owe the rest of his amiable team at Destiny Image Europe! I will not easily forget his words during one of those preliminary phone calls: "You are anointed to write, and we are anointed to publish." That's a veritable Kingdom network! Indeed, the Lord has given the word, and, as we would usually say at The Preacher®, "great" is "the company" of those who publish it (see Ps. 68:11).

I am also indebted to our dedicated partners worldwide on The Preacher® Team, whose commitment to the vision and passion to spread the blessing has accomplished the publication of this volume.

Finally, to the staff—full time and volunteers—in the ministry office of The Preacher®, I pray as well for you, that the Lord will strengthen your hands for more, that He will remember you and do you good in your day, and that you may not miss your contact person who should take you into your chamber of prepared glory. The accursed serpent of Melita shall never write the last chapter of your precious lives.

A Word from the Author

The Preacher® is the name of a prophetic Pen as well as a will-ing "company" of publishers (see Psalm 68:11) which the Lord has raised up to ink that pen and circulate the words of its prophecies around the globe, especially in print and also by radio and on the web. In the past three decades, like a voice in the wilderness, this epistolary ministry has regularly published millions of bulletins, magazines, and books on various aspects of the Christian life, such as intercession, spiritual warfare, righteousness and holiness, Christian leadership, etc., all of which have been acclaimed best sellers and have served to inspire countless readers, among them notable leaders of the global Church. That Voice, on occasion, has served as the prophetic watch to which so many have looked for the guiding star that would lead to the manger of divine purpose where God's next *move* lies concealed from the learned and the strong.

The Lord declares in Matthew 23:34, "Behold, I send unto you prophets, and wise men, and scribes." God sends not only *prophets* and *wise men* but also *scribes*. This "sent" prophetic scribe has had to mail scrolls and parchments across the globe and speak and teach in conferences around the world, proclaiming the Word from on high.

Contents

Preface

This juicy volume is essentially a reviewed compilation of earlier, smaller publications by The Preacher Press®, Nigeria, which have appeared under their respective chapter titles. They line up here under the theme "Encounters." These would be those encounters by which God draws us into His workshop to make us, after which He sends us forth to display us, as well as the challenges that threaten to humiliate us in the process of cautiously walking the path of that glory.

The stitching together of those random volumes into a nobler garment presented a fresh challenge—by what most appropriate democratic title should this republic of independent epistles be called? That is every writer's infrequent pen-ache, even the best of them. Sometimes, a title seems to float to you effortlessly and fits perfectly into place. At other times, you have to carve and chisel from this construction and that until some piece fits better than the rest.

When Destiny Image Europe suggested this novel portmanteau of apparently divergent publications, I must admit I found the challenge daunting. My reluctance was that of a schoolboy, who, having just finished preparation for a long-dreamed-of vacation, is told to repeat a past homework assignment instead. But now! How sweet the vista seems!

Each of these volumes was a best seller when it first appeared, or at least that is what numerous reviews declared. It was quite encouraging, therefore, when the preliminary review from Destiny Image Europe stated in rather superlative terms, "We found the message in each booklet *very* interesting and *most* importantly tailored *in an intelligent way* to build the faith of each believer." For that, we are thankful to God, and trust that you, too, will find this book no less inspiring and edifying than the hundreds of those who have so testified over the years.

Welcome to the Potter's House for the breaking processes that should bring the best out of you. But be ready, too, for the path that leads beyond that re-creation chamber, through the dreary seas, and on to the shores of greater glory. Amen.

The Preacher®
October 2009

SECTION ONE

POINTERS TO THE POTTER'S HOUSE

Introduction

Life is the product of those we meet and those we miss. Every "today" is the product of past encounters and opportunities met or missed. In the journey of life, destiny often charts our course into encounters that should bring us to a determined place. To miss those encounters is to wander aimlessly through the rest of life, awaiting the grave. However, there are some encounters we are better off without. What if Samson had been other than where Delilah found him on the day he was fated to lose his vision? (See Judges 16.) What if Ahab had never married Jezebel? (See 1 Kings 16:29-34.) And what if the young prophet had not slowed down enough to be caught and tricked by the fatal old prophet in the incident with Jeroboam? (See 1 Kings 13.) Is there an encounter in your life that you would have been better off without?

Just as those on satanic assignment are not likely to appear in the stereotypical horned and hoofed devil costumes, angels divinely sent to take us into the place of our glory will probably not come adorned in white robes or with halos above their humble heads. They might appear as simple servants characterized by their jars of service. (See Luke 22:10.) And yet, anyone who chooses to ignore them will do so at their own peril. They are not the destination, but they are a sure link to the destination. After all, the value of a key is not in its decorated looks. It is in the doors it opens.

After Saul was anointed king of Israel, the prophet Samuel advised him that he still needed to have three consecutive vital contacts that would impact his life in significant ways. The anointing alone was not all that was needed. (See 1 Samuel 10:1-4.) There is much that the Potter will do in each of us, but often, He needs someone to get us into position. That is like the captivating first chapter of an open-ended book, with a possibility of plots heading in several directions.

CHAPTER 1

The Man You Must Not Miss

VITAL CONTACTS

Recently, I had an invitation to speak at a church. As I sat there waiting to be called up, it occurred to me that I was in that place because of the secretary we had hired in our missionary office two years before. Through her, I had come to know her elder brother, and through him, I had been invited to speak to that congregation. For that reason, whatever happened during or through the meeting that night—say a bomb had gone off, or the people I met there turned out to be friends or enemies, or I met a friend who introduced me to a king—it would all have been because two years before I had met someone. That encounter put me on the path to where I ended up that night. If the Lord had said to me in the beginning, "Hire her" or "Don't hire her," I would not have known all the reasons why. It would not necessarily have been because she was a good or bad person, a skilled or unskilled secretary. It would largely have been because God saw the future and knew our meeting was going to chart the course of my life in ways I would never have suspected at the time.

You yourself are where you are now, and you are reading this book now, because of some contact you have had in the past. Your spouse, the schools you attended, your job, where you live—all these are products of contacts you've had in the past. Similarly, your "tomorrow" will be the product of those you meet or miss "today." In fact, every "today" is the product of many encounters in the past and many opportunities found or lost yesterday.

In the journey of life, there comes a time when destiny charts a person's course to cross the path of another, occasioning an encounter that should catapult that person into a prepared, ordained place. To miss that encounter is to wander aimlessly through the rest of life, waiting merely for the grave.

Joseph's journey from the place of his dreams (his father's tent) to the place of the fulfillment of those dreams (Pharaoh's palace) was marked by many such encounters, several of them disguised as challenges. What is perhaps the first significant encounter was with the nameless guide who pointed the way to his brothers, who had been scheming murderously to be done with him. (See Genesis 37:15-17.) Another encounter was with Mrs. Potiphar, who falsely accused him and had him sent to jail where strangely, he was to meet the last contact—a man who would bring him into the palace of Egypt. (See Genesis 39:21.) These were divine connections disguised as challenges and hardship.

The steps of a good man, indeed, are *ordered by the Lord*, but that doesn't eliminate the storms on the sea and the stones in the way (see Ps. 37:23). In fact, those threats constitute a reason why He is there— to *order* the steps. Even when the Lord is the Shepherd, the journey still runs into detours at times. While passing through "the valley of the shadow of death," we are still able to say "Thou art with me" (Ps. 23:4). The paths that lead to our treasure house are not all paved with gold and strewn with roses. If the seductive and malicious Mrs. Potiphar could be Joseph's vital contact to the throne, then those whom Heaven has ordained to guide us to the place of our destiny will not all be angels. Think of it this way: the Master Himself had given the instruction, "Let us go over," and He Himself was there in the boat on that mission, yet there arose a great storm that threatened the trip. But thanks be to God, He never sends us across alone. When He said, "Let us go," He was right there with them (Mark 4:35 NIV).

"Jesus came and spoke to them, saying, 'All authority has been given to Me....Go therefore...and lo, I am with you always.' Amen" (Matt. 28:18-20 NKJV). He never sends us out and stays behind. He is the coach who not only trains us but also gets into the ring with us. (See Daniel 3:19-27.)

Divine connections do not rule out the possibility of terminative snares—Mrs. Potiphar, the seductress; Judas, the double agent; Sanballat, the sworn enemy; and Goliath the giant. Divine guidance and God's presence, however, make all the difference. After all, it took an opportunity disguised as the terrifying giant Goliath to advertise and exalt the young David overnight. God was in it. When God is there, even dangerous situations become divine arrangements for connecting us to our promotion.

Sometimes the guide to our place of destiny is a sign that God places before us, a sign that everyone else sees but fails to understand. For the Israelites on their way to the Promised Land, it was the pillar of cloud by day and a pillar of fire by night. (See Exodus 13:21-22.) For the wise men on their way to worship the newborn King, it was a star in the sky, the significance of which even the residents of the town of Bethlehem failed to grasp. (See Matthew 2.) And in that memorable first Easter season, everyone in the crowded judgment hall heard the cock crow, but only Peter understood what it meant that morning. (See Mark 14:66-72.) Every sign does not speak to every person.

The Man With the Jar

When the time approached for His last Passover feast on earth, Jesus told His disciples how to locate the house and the host for the crucial ceremony.

"As you enter the city, a man carrying a jar of water will meet you. Follow him to the house that he enters, and say to the owner of the house, 'The Teacher asks: Where is the guest room, where I may eat the Passover with my disciples?' He will show you a large upper room, all furnished. Make preparations there." They left and found things just as Jesus had told them. So they prepared the Passover (Luke 22:10-13, NIV).

The disciples were on a mission to an unfamiliar place where they were to be met by a man with a jar. He would be their prophetic pointer to their goal. It's possible the man was not even aware that he was Heaven's signpost to some travelers sent by God in the journey of life. If the disciples had missed the man with the jar, they would have missed their part in God's wonderful plan of redemption.

BEYOND THE ANOINTING

After Saul's first anointing as king over Israel, he was told by the prophet Samuel that he would have three consecutive vital encounters that would impact his life in significant ways. The anointing had merely been an ignition to propel him on his way to those contacts.

Samuel took a vial of oil, and poured it upon his head, and kissed him, and said, Is it not because the Lord hath anointed thee to be captain over His inheritance? When thou art departed from me to day, then thou shalt find two men by Rachel's sepulchre in the border of Benjamin at Zelzah; and they will say unto thee, The asses which thou wentest to seek are found: and, lo, thy father hath left the care of the asses, and sorroweth for you, saying, What shall I do for my son? Then shalt thou go on forward from thence, and thou shalt come to the plain of Tabor, and there shall meet thee three men going up to God to Bethel, one carrying three kids, and another carrying three loaves of bread, and another carrying a bottle of wine: And they will salute thee, and give thee two loaves of bread; which thou shalt receive of their hands (1 Samuel 10:1-4).

His first contact was going to be with two men who were going to give him the vital *information* that the asses for which he had been searching were found and his father had begun to be concerned about him. That was information that should soothe his heart which was beginning to ache with concern. That was going to be a ministration to his *soul*.

Not everyone has money to give, but everyone has something to give. Information is no less vital than goods. Today, information is a very expensive commodity. Some contacts are for meeting an emotional need. Anointed men also have their share of emotional needs. The anointing does not erase their humanity (or human frailty).

Next, Saul was going to meet three men who were going to offer him *material support*. The men would give him two out of the three loaves of bread they had brought along on their journey. Unlike the previous contact, they were going to minister essentially to his *body*. The anointing on him was going to begin to attract favor, and he would not have to lobby for it. The further Saul went down the path of God, the more contacts would be there to minister to him—first *two* men, then *three* men, and then a *company* of prophets.

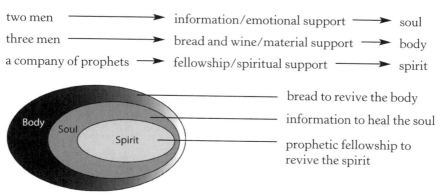

Not everyone is meant to minister to your soul. Not everyone has been endowed to give the same type of support. Not everyone feels your heartbeat enough to address your emotional needs.

Some people are not equipped to provide ministering words, but rather material support and a greeting. Often, these people go out of their way to give.

There is a time when gifts should not be received, as when Gehazi pursued Naaman's gifts against the counsel of his master, Elisha, and caught leprosy in the process. (See 2 Kings 5.) But there is also a time when gifts should not be refused. It certainly seems unfair that one man and his servant should be given two of the three loaves while three adult men still on their journey are left with just one. But God had said that the newly anointed king was not to reject the offer. (See 1 Samuel 10:3-4.) It didn't matter how anyone felt. They greeted him, establishing a contact and making an acquaintance. Then they gave him bread to strengthen him on his way. It was also a gift of *relationship*. Some relationships are worth more than money can buy.

The third contact was to be with a group of prophets who would offer much more than the material and secular support the previous contacts had provided. They would minister to his *spirit*. Their company would ignite the latent spiritual powers resident in him since his anointing. Their mission in his life would be essentially *spiritual*.

> *After that thou shalt come to the hill of God, where is the garrison of the Philistines: and it shall come to pass, when thou art come thither to the city, that thou shalt meet a company of prophets coming down from the high place with a psaltery, and a tabret, and a pipe, and a harp, before them; and they shall prophesy: And the Spirit of the Lord will come upon thee, and thou shalt prophesy with them, and shalt be turned into another man (1 Samuel 10:5-6).*

Saul had already been anointed, yet the Spirit of God was going to come upon him in a different and greater fashion once he made contact with the company of prophets. He had been anointed, but now he would be transformed into a different man, one with the potential to prophesy. This would be ignited by yet another unique encounter that would manifest that grace in his life.

Regardless of how much oil is poured on our heads, some abilities in us will not be expressed until we have an encounter with the "man you must not miss." If we miss this destined contact or company, there are some spiritual depths we will never reach.

There are some people, though anointed, who might never prophesy because they missed the specific prophetic company that should have stirred that gift in them. Today they are not where they should be, because they missed the man who should have taken them there.

In the Book of Acts, chapter 3, we read the story of a man whose family placed him every morning at the gate of the temple, known to everyone as the Beautiful Gate, to beg alms. Born lame, the pleasant name of the gate mocked his ugly condition. Multitudes passed by him every day of his life, but none could take him beyond that begging post where his disability had anchored him until two disciples, Peter and John, came his way. They spoke the words that restored strength to his crippled bones and extended their hands to pull him up onto his feet. After his encounter with Peter and John, the man began to jump and leap in and out of the temple. Those entering the temple on that day recognized the man as the beggar to whom they had thrown a few coins of pity through the years. That was the best they could do. It took an encounter with Peter and John to raise him up and give him a new life.

But what would have happened if the lame man's family had dropped him off late on that particular day after Peter and John had already gone inside? What if they had missed each other? This would have been a good story never told. Regardless of how generous people might have been with their alms, the man would have remained a cripple, even though Heaven had made plans for him to go jumping and leaping through the rest of his life.

YOUR LINK TO DESTINY

There are some contacts in life, though you might never recognize them all, that are ordained by God to bring you to your "prepared place," the place of the feast, or your "large upper room, all furnished." If you should miss them, you will have missed your destiny. They might not be clothed in purple robes. They might be simple servants characterized by their jar or pitcher of service, but you will ignore them to your perpetual peril. They are not your destination, but they are your sure link to your destination. Being merely servants, they might look on the surface as if it is they who are in need of you, as if your relationship with them would make a demand on your purse. But you would need them more than they would ever need you. God sends you to them not for their sake but for yours. After all, it was a servant, even a nameless servant, who first recommended the absent David to the palace of King Saul. (See 1 Samuel 16:18.)

In a season of acute and widespread famine, God sent the prophet Elijah to a widow in the town of Zarephath. (See 1 Kings 17:8-17.) Was it merely for the widow's sake? True, she benefited from and was sustained by the prophet's company throughout the famine, but it could be argued that the prophet needed her much more. The widow had already resigned herself to death, after all. But Elijah needed not only her well prepared meals but also her caring, motherly company and the accommodation she offered in that foreign land. What if he had missed her? What if she had missed him?

Is God sending you to a little village church? It might not be just for the sake of the church, but for your sake as well. Perhaps that is where you would meet your spouse, the person you have been searching for all these years. Maybe some UNICEF project will take that person to that village, where you will be seen as a shining jewel in that humble place, and you will be chosen as a cherished spouse. You could then see that God had sent you there not only for the villagers' sake but also for your own. Perhaps a little boy you will meet and convert to Christ in that place will one day become the governor of a state and will provide you with special favor at some point in the future, as well as being an asset for the Kingdom. God would have been sending you there for your own sake as well as that of others.

A graduate brother chose a simple round hut in a little missionary village for his mandatory one-year, post-graduation National Youth Service assignment in Nigeria. There he met a German girl who had chosen to come to the country as a missionary. She wanted to be married to a Nigerian Christian and reasoned that whoever she might find on such a mission field would be a Christian indeed.

The young man's colleagues mocked him when they heard where he intended to live in order to be close to the people he wanted to reach. But it was his round hut, the one his city-friends despised, that first attracted the German missionary girl. Today they are married with children and serving God in Germany.

No one gets a German visa from a village hut, but that is where God sent this young man to get his. Others have sought the same visa in vain from the German embassy in the big capital city. But this young man, faithful to God in his little round hut, freely received all he needed and more. Like the royal Star over Bethlehem, everyone else saw it, but only the shepherds and the Wise Men followed it to the Christ Child.

Lessons From an Ex-Slave

David, the anointed fugitive on the run from King Saul with his band of soldiers, got back home to camp one day and found a disaster. A marauding gang of Amalekites had invaded and looted their camp, carrying away all their wives and children. David's men were in a panic, but David received the counsel of God, and they left in pursuit of the Amalekites. On the way, they came upon a half-dead Egyptian slave, whose master was a captain of the gang that had invaded and looted David's camp at Ziklag. He told David and his men, "My master abandoned me when I became ill three days ago" (1 Sam. 30:13 NIV). The captain-master discarded the poor, sick slave boy because he had become an unexpected liability. He had no idea that such a lowly boy held the key to his own survival. Wallowing as it were in the intoxicating nature of his present prosperity, he could never have imagined that he could be brought low by such a despicable, dispensable dying slave (see 1 Sam. 30:1-31).

When David found that dying slave boy, he saw in him something the boy's ex-master completely overlooked—the link to his recovery of the looted treasures and their abducted family members. He was "the man with the jar." David saved that slave boy's life and then let him lead them to the place where the feasting Amalekites were sprawled in the plain, celebrating their recent booty. David routed them and recovered everyone and everything they had taken from his camp. The foolish Amalekites auctioned their "tomorrow" when they abandoned the slave boy "yesterday." And though their "today" shone with promise of riches and pleasure, it would not last. Their oversight was David's divine connection. But what if David had missed the boy? David was already an anointed soldier with a mandate from God upon his life for that mission, but had he missed that boy, he might have searched much longer than God intended.

Has the enemy stolen from you? I pray that God will bring you to the vital contact that will cause you to recover everything you have lost. Be watchful and discerning. The "slave" or humble person you disregard today could be the key to your future. Do what you can in accordance with your conscience.

LESSONS FROM CONTEMPORARY LIFE

Imagine for a moment that there were two friends—one a trader and the other a preacher. The preacher knew nothing of trade, yet it was casual information from the preacher and contacts received through him that made the trader a millionaire. They always said they had no idea why God would have brought them together so many years before.

Now imagine a Christian manager who has a female secretary. The secretary's husband is a driver for a multinational corporation. One day, the secretary falls ill and is hospitalized. Her husband visits her and brings along his boss, the head of the corporation. The Christian manager is there visiting as well. The two bosses strike up a conversation that leads to a relationship, which in turn leads to millions of dollars of business for the Christian manager.

That manager had hired the secretary out of kindness because she needed a job, but in the end it was she who gave him jobs. She turned out to be to him "the man with the jar," his divine contact to the business breakthroughs he'd always prayed for. Had he missed making that crucial connection or sacked his secretary because she fell sick, he would have remained static and poorer for the rest of his life. Her husband was a mere driver. He was no multinational businessman, but he was the key to the Christian manager's multinational businesses. Like his wife, he too was "the man with the jar."

A Christian woman, a widow, woke up one morning with a strange urge to drive across town to have breakfast at a certain restaurant. After struggling with the feeling for some time, she gave in and drove to the restaurant. The man across the breakfast table from her was a widower who had been praying for God to send him the right partner. They got married shortly after. The restaurant was not her destination. It was merely her "man with the jar," her link to her destination. Had she disregarded the seemingly pointless urge to go to breakfast, she would never have known what she missed—a divine connection.

God causes certain people to cross our paths at opportune times in order to positively affect our lives. These people might not be great in themselves, but they hold the key to our greatness. The value of a key is not in its decorated looks; it is in the doors it can open. An insignificant little key can open the door to great possibilities.

The jar-bearers God brings your way most likely won't be wearing kingly robes or halos above their humble heads. Rainbows won't decorate the sky to let you know you are about to meet one, so be watchful and discerning. Never dismiss anyone because of their looks and don't make the mistake of thinking only kings and queens and princes are capable of taking you into your palace of greatness. Joseph, assistant to pharaoh and ex-prisoner, would testify that divine connections often come disguised—sometimes as fellow prisoners! No, God doesn't usually choose kings to lead us to our thrones. Besides, not all kings are found in palaces. Some are concealed in mangers, far from the view of subtle and deadly nobles. Ask the Wise Men from the East. (See Matthew 2:2-12.)

That fellow you ignore because he was born in a manger could be a king—the king for whom the ages have been waiting. He might be a king that your eyes are unable to see, whereas strangers from distant lands stream down to worship him. May satanic agents, seeing a star you cannot see, not follow him up to make him, tomorrow, an antichrist; twice the son of hell than they are themselves. (See Matthew 23:14.)

Richard Wurmbrand, in his book *Was Karl Marx a Satanist?*, says that Karl Marx, who was one of the intellectual bastions of the antichrist philosophy of communism, once considered himself a Christian. In the course of his career, he met a teacher who influenced his thoughts. In the end, he became a satanist and fueled the communist cause that sent millions to hell. If only his priests had known what he was going to become, perhaps they might have watched more carefully over his soul.

I was shocked to learn that a young man who grew up in the same church I did and twenty years earlier had professed to be a Christian had adopted an Islamic identity in Nigeria and turned out lately to be an armed threat to the national peace. Others of us grew up to become ministers of the Gospel, but he became a terrorist. Nobody could have known so many years ago what the future would make of that little boy. If we could, perhaps everyone would have held more closely to him.

Treasure Disguised in a Leper's House

Naaman, the leprous general of the Syrian army, was a great man respected by his king. He was a noble man in the class of kings. But the person who held the key to his recovery from the shameful disease of leprosy was his little slave maid. It was information he received from her that led him to the place of his recovery—a miracle he had searched for and failed to find in all the great places he had gone to for answers. (See 2 Kings 5:2-3.) If Naaman or his wife had been abusing and mistreating that little girl, she might never have provided the key to their mutual joy.

Is it possible that your present domestic help is destined for your future good, although she seems to you now an inconvenient dependent slave? Could the previous slave you ill-treated until she fled for her life have been sent to rescue your children from the fire disaster in which they died a month after she was gone?

We cannot deny that satan also has "men with a jar," agents sent into homes as servants to bring about satanic contacts intended to frustrate those families from reaching their God-ordained destiny. But that is not to say that everyone is an agent of satan. Besides, the light shines *in darkness*, and the darkness does not comprehend it (see John 1:5).

A Nigerian family had a housemaid whom they treated well, not as a second-class citizen as is often the case in some great homes. She became a part of the family. In due course, she married an expatriate Indian friend of the family. Years later, things got very bad for the Nigerian family. They could hardly feed themselves. Their ex-maid turned out to be their only significant lifeline. If they had been evil to her, she might never have met their Indian friend, and they would never have known the support that she became. It was a mutual link.

TIMING

Suppose the two disciples that Jesus sent to find the room had chosen to wait a day or two before making the journey, would they still have met the man with the jar? Suppose the widow we spoke about earlier in this book had chosen to go for dinner rather than breakfast that day? Suppose she had decided to go to breakfast on a different day? She would still have been obeying the divine instruction, but her delay would have nullified God's intention.

Had the two disciples set out on the path of obedience a day later, they would have considered themselves still on God's mission, but they would have missed the man with the jar. They would have missed, as Jesus said of Jerusalem, the *time* of their visitation (See Luke 19:41-44.) They might have found many other men carrying many jars, but none of them would have been ordained to bring them to the prepared place. It would have all ended in confusion. It was not just about the place and the person they were to meet; there was also a time to the pattern.

30

Some of the confusion that besets us today is the result of yesterday's disobedience or delay.

LOCATIONS

What if the disciples had gone to a different city rather than the one Jesus sent them to? Would they there have found the man with the jar? No! They would have missed him. Jesus didn't choose that city because it was great, He chose it because the divine connection—the man with the jar—was there. What if they had decided the city Jesus sent them to was not famous enough or important enough, so they went somewhere else. They might have enjoyed the greatness and fame of the city of their choice, but they would have missed the man with the jar. They might have found another man or even several men with jars—but they would have only been a distraction and would not have led the disciples to a prepared place of miracles.

Distractions are usually very glamorous, otherwise they would have no power to distract. Very often, they appear more attractive than the true object of our divine mission. Error is not always totally wrong, which is why it ensnares.

God does not perform every miracle in every place. Some places are unique for the things that prophecy will accomplish there. A time came when God had a special message for the prophet Jeremiah. God could not deliver it in every place. The prophet had to get to an agreed location to be able to contact and receive that message. (See Jeremiah 18:2.)

RELOCATING FOR THE ENCOUNTER

To be where the man with the jar would meet them, the disciples had to leave where they were, which also meant leaving their friends and colleagues and going to another place. To be *located* properly for that divine encounter, they had to *relocate*. To relocate, they had to be *dislocated* from their *past* location. Relocation is the product of dislocation, which could sometimes be a great sacrifice.

After Abram set out from Ur of the Chaldees on his way to Canaan, he could not receive the fullness of the seven blessings due him until he had been totally dislocated from his roots. His nephew, Lot, who was traveling with him, served as a lingering symbol of Abram's haunting past. (See Genesis 12:1-5;13:14.) The seven blessings were dependent on a willing dislocation from three levels of affinity: his country, his kindred, and his father's house.

> *The Lord had said unto Abram, Get thee out of thy country, and from thy kindred, and from thy father's house, unto a land that I will shew thee: And* [there] [1] ***I will make of thee a great nation,*** *and* [2] ***I will bless thee,*** *and* [3] ***make thy name great;*** *and* [4] ***thou shalt be a blessing:*** *And* [5] ***I will bless them that bless thee,*** *and* [6] ***curse him that curseth thee:*** *and* [7] ***in thee shall all families of the earth be blessed.*** *So Abram departed, as the Lord had spoken unto him; and Lot* [his nephew, representing his "father's house"] *went with him* (Genesis 12:1-4).

Some time later, we read:

> *The Lord said unto Abram,* **after that Lot was separated from him,** *Lift up* **now** *thine eyes, and look from the place where thou art northward, and southward, and eastward, and westward: For all the land which thou seest, to thee will I give it, and to thy seed for ever. And I will make thy seed as the dust of the earth: so that if a man can number the dust of the earth, then shall thy seed also be numbered* (Genesis 13:14-16).

Being in the right place involves leaving the wrong place. The wrong place never becomes right, no matter how much it might be decorated, even with the "right" people. To be anywhere, one has to leave somewhere else. When God says for you to move, do so. Do not expect the man with the jar to meet you where you are not.

ACCORDING TO THE PATTERN

Before God commissioned Moses to build the tabernacle in the wilderness, He showed him a pattern of the heavenly tabernacle. Moses was instructed to ensure that the earthly model was *according to the pattern* that had been shown him. (See Exodus 25:40.) For every mission, God always gives a pattern.

Suppose the disciples had begun to *interrogate* rather than *follow* the man with the jar when they found him, that would have been contrary to the "pattern" they had been shown, and they would have confused him or aroused his suspicion. The instruction was for them to follow him until he had led them to the house, and then to ask about his boss.

It is important not only to hear clearly but also to follow divine instructions carefully. Otherwise you could indeed find the man with the jar and still ruin the mission.

HE MAY NEVER KNOW

Was the man with the jar aware of the mission that God had placed upon him? No. He was fulfilling a mission without realizing it. That is why he was to be followed silently. On that mission, there was a time to follow silently, and a time and place to speak. There is a time for everything. (See Ecclesiastes 3:1.)

The "man" that God is sending forth to be a sign to you may never know that he is a sign. Yet his not knowing it makes little difference to the fact.

THEY WENT, THEY FOUND

"They went, and found *as* he had said unto them…" (Luke 22:13 NKJV). They obeyed, and then they found the result of their obedience. Several of us would rather see a sign before we obey, but the sign will be found in our obedience. Ten lepers met Jesus, asking to be healed. Jesus told them to go and show themselves to the priest. It was "as they went" that "they were cleansed" of their leprosy. They were healed as they obeyed (Luke 17:14).

SUSTAINING RELATIONSHIPS

Suppose the disciples had antagonized the man with the jar when they first found him. Do you think he would have been willing to answer them when they later needed information from him? I doubt it. Suppose they had flaunted their eminent "discipleship" in the face of that ordinary, simple servant. Would they have found him later when they needed him? I doubt it.

Let us be meek in this regard. We might need the help of another person tomorrow in spite of where we might find that person today. Many, through their un-Christlike conduct, have ruined relationships that God meant for their future good. Sadly, many of them will never even realize what they have forever lost. Some masters and mistresses have badly treated their servants and employees, thereby ruining relationships that God had intended for their own future good.

Some servants, on the other hand, exploit the love and trust of their masters and have defrauded them of money. In the process, they have closed the door to the honest dollars their masters could have provided for them for their faithful service. Today they celebrate a prodigal's paltry glory, whereas they have lost much more than they will ever know.

Had Joseph abused his master's trust and succumbed to the seductions of the master's unfaithful wife, he could have been elevated *in her house,* perhaps to the rank of "chief superior servant," or "kitchen headmaster." But while he might have enjoyed that "promotion," he would have missed the glory that faithfulness brought him as Prime Minister of the whole kingdom of Egypt.

Alas, how many people today fit this picture? Some could have become prime minister of their kingdom, but instead were derailed, perhaps for life, by a distracting premature promotion earned through compromise. They have ended up as the domesticated prime ministers of Mrs. Potiphar's kitchen!

Mrs. Potiphar was intended by satan as a vital contact to ruin Joseph's path to glory. His intent was to disguise the treachery as favor, love, and promotion. Through Joseph's tenacious faithfulness to God, however, that cunning snare was converted into a vital contact for his ultimate true promotion. (See Genesis 39.) Joseph remained true to his absent master even when he had good opportunity to do otherwise. The fact that his ungrateful master repaid his loyalty by having him thrown in jail changed nothing. Joseph acted to defend his master's honor out of his own sense of integrity, knowing God would reward him in due time.

The master you defraud and alienate today may have been ordained by God to save you tomorrow. Had Gehazi served Elisha faithfully to the end as Elisha had served Elijah, Gehazi might have received the double portion of Elisha's anointing that Elisha received from Elijah. But greed and the lure of quick gain brought a promising relationship to an abrupt leprous end. (See 2 Kings 5.) He pursued what seemed to him a noble contact, a quick bridge to the future he had always dreamed of. He abused the contact. He betrayed his master and defrauded the nobleman. For his actions, he was cursed with leprosy. It is believed by some scholars that the four famous lepers outside the city gates of Samaria who announced the discovered abundance of food in the deserted camp of the Syrians at the height of their city's famine were Gehazi and his three sons. (See 2 Kings 7:3-20.)

Servants should ensure that they do not waste the gift of a relationship. The master you are exploiting today could be your "future" disguised. Today you are satisfied with a few stolen hundreds from his purse, but too late you may realize that he could have made you the millionaire you were meant to become—if only you had waited and had been faithful.

CHAPTER 2

Becoming the Man With the Jar

NOT EXPLOITING RELATIONSHIPS

One day a stranger, after conferring with her husband, confronted the prophet Elisha with a great gesture that he could not refuse—a transit room on his prophetic routes. He turned out also to be her miracle, for it was by his intervention that the lingering yoke of her barrenness was broken.

In the acceptance speech by which the prophet made her the reciprocal offer through his servant, he said this, "You have gone to all this trouble for us. Now what can be done for you? Can we speak on your behalf to the king or the commander of the army?" (2 Kings 4:13 NIV).

This suggests that Elisha had strong connections with those in power. He had great influence over the king and the political and military leadership in the land. Still, he remained in need of the simple accommodation of the transit room the woman and her husband so kindly offered him. They had long been observing his silent need. The prophet had those powerful connections, but he would never use them to his own advantage. He could use the contacts to help others, but not to promote himself.

Do not exploit relationships. Do not try to make a "man with a jar" out of another person if God has not said so. In 1 Corinthians 9:2-17, Paul acknowledged his right to receive material gifts from those to whom he had offered spiritual gifts, but he said that it was a right he would not exploit, for the Gospel's sake. Unlike him, many have ruined relationships by using their power over others for personal gain.

In our society today, many male university lecturers, for example, sexually exploit their female students who are often desperate for undeserved pass grades. They do not know who those girls might someday become, so they exploit the relationships and in many cases, seal their own future for the worse. Heartless landlords have also ruined potential relationships with their tenants, by exploiting them when they are powerless to speak up for themselves. Like Esau, many have sold their future for a plate of pottage; a future they would *tearfully* seek tomorrow, but in vain. "For ye know how that afterward, when he would have inherited the blessing, he was rejected: for he found no place of repentance, though he sought it carefully with tears" (Heb. 12:17).

If God makes you a prophet over a people or over a king and his army general, it is not for you to exploit the privilege for your greedy, pompous, and ambitious advantage.

Two years before his miracle was due, Joseph tried to use his contact with a staff in Pharaoh's palace to get himself out of God's training camp, also known as an unjust jail term. It didn't work out. When the time came, however, without any effort on his part, he was ushered into his "furnished upper room," as prime minister in a foreign land. (See Genesis 40:14; 41:1, 9-14.)

A SAD CASE

The Kenyan preacher John Chacha told a story that has never left me. One day in a Kenyan supermarket, the Lord drew his attention to a young man who needed the Gospel. He walked over to the young man and began to speak to him, but that fellow had no time for God. He would give in to no entreaty. As that young man stubbornly walked away from John Chacha to cross the street, he was hit by a speeding truck and killed. It was such a bad accident that, according to the story, they had to scoop his flesh from the asphalt surface in some places.

God saw the end had come for that nameless young man, so He sent a preacher his way. His intention was to give him both *long life* (so that he would not die that day) and *eternal life* (so that he would not go to hell). If he had received that preacher with the "jar" of Gospel water, he might well have been spared. Regrettably, he missed it—to his eternal misery. Had he been listening to the preacher, the truck that killed him would have passed by while he was still drinking the life-giving water from the preacher's Gospel jar. Even if he had failed to repent, and so missed eternal life, at least he would have lived longer. Unfortunately, that day he missed both long life and eternal life.

Have you yet made a decision to be born again? If not, may I be your "man with a jar" to offer you life and eternity? Get down on your knees. Pray. May yours not be another sad story but a joyous one of salvation.

DISCERNING THE MAN

There is a place already prepared for the feast, and only one man can get us there. Yet in the course of our walk, we daily encounter people who are distractions and add no value to our lives. Only God can open our eyes to see the man with the jar in the midst of those distractions. The prayer to pray at this point is, "Lord, open my eyes."

I pray that God will open our eyes to discern the man with the jar. May we not miss that vital contact that God has arranged to bring us into our prepared place.

CARRY A JAR YOURSELF

In our selfish world, most people look out for themselves, each determining what advantage he or she can gain from another. Fewer are those who seek out ways to enhance the lives of others. Don't try to make a jar-carrier of every man or woman you meet. Carry a jar filled with the nourishing water of life yourself and add value to someone else's life.

BOUGHT THROUGH FORGIVENESS

A bishop friend of mine bought a very large piece of land on which to build his church. After paying more than twenty million naira (more than $130,000.00) for the land, he realized they had been paying the money to the wrong person. The land belonged to a community and was actually part of a much larger tract of land already purchased by a large firm. The negotiations had been on to tidy up the deal.

One day, he was in church when three men walked in. One was the white expatriate boss of the firm that had bought the land. One was their indigenous Nigerian manager. The third was the chairman of the landlord community. The bishop's land and the big church cathedral on it were in danger of being forfeited.

The chairman spoke up right away. After introducing his colleagues, he asked, "You do not remember me, do you?"

The bishop could not remember meeting him.

The chairman continued. "A few years ago, there was an accident involving my car and yours. I was at fault. Your driver was very frightened and insisted that I follow him to see his boss and explain the accident myself. When we got into your house, you were engrossed with a program on the TV. After hearing your driver, with your face still glued to the TV, you merely asked, 'Was anyone injured? Is anyone dead?' When the answer was 'No,' you simply said, 'I forgive you. Go.' You did not turn back to see my face. You did not even go out to see the extent of the damage to your car.

"This land belongs to my community. The firm for which these two men work has already purchased it from us. But I told them that they could not have your portion of the land because this church was our own community church. Here are the documents for your land, all duly processed. I was that man who hit your car, the man you forgave—and now I give what I can to you."

The land stayed. It had been paid for by forgiveness. This was truly a divine connection. When God brought about their contact years before in the form of an auto accident, the bishop could not have known that he was buying his future with the "currency" of his forgiveness. God was giving him the land for his headquarters church. In this case, the man with the jar was disguised. Had the bishop insisted back then on collecting what was due him, he would have lost more—much more, and he probably would never have known it. He gave forgiveness and received his miracle.

REMEMBERED BY WHAT YOU HAVE DONE

Fading away like the stars of the morning,
Losing their light in the glorious day,
Thus would we pass from the earth and its toiling,
Only remembered by what we have done.
(H. Bonar D.D.)

You are the product of other people's input. Where are the products of your inputs? Even if you were the result of someone's wrong input, you should make a difference in another's life. You will be remembered not so much for what you were given as for what you gave; not so much for how much money you made as for the people you made. Begin to add value to others' lives. Carry a jar that identifies you to others as the person to follow to the "prepared places."

41

There is a man you must not miss. I pray that God will order your steps to that vital contact for your promotion. But I pray also that you will become the man or woman for God (not for satan) that somebody else must never miss, the man with the jar, someone else's divine connection to greatness.

In the words of Bonar's hymn, may it be said again that after everything else has faded away into eternity "like the stars of the morning," you will be remembered by what you have done. What will that be?

SECTION TWO

WELCOME TO THE POTTER'S HOUSE

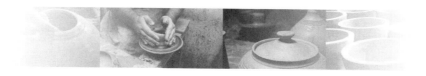

Introduction

God ordains contacts of various sorts to bring us into the place of His purpose, where He might do His work in us and through us. God receives us as we are, but if we let Him, He does not leave us as we are. He goes to work, and He's still at work, changing lives. The Master takes no Sabbath until His work is done. None are beyond divine re-creation who would let the Potter perfect His purpose in them.

Jesus said to His disciples, "Follow Me, and I will make you…" This has taught me often to say, "You are made by whom you follow" (Matt. 4:19). As we found in Chapter One, Saul began to prophesy when he found himself in the company of prophesying men. Everyone is the product of those whom they follow. It is also commonly said, "Show me your friends, and I will tell you who you are."

The process and duration of the making, however, differs from follower to follower, and from maker to maker, depending on several factors. Joseph had to be separated from his loving father and thrown into prison in a foreign land before he could be made into the man who would save his generation. The same was true of Moses, who had his de-Egyptianization in the "back side" of the Midian desert. It took a war with Saul, the backslidden tyrant, to make David into the great leader he later became. Elisha received his double portion by following Elijah through to the point of the impartation. For Elisha, it was close to a decade. For Joseph, thirteen years, and for Moses, it took forty years.

It would appear, however, that there are things that destiny will not accomplish merely by a one-time fortuitous contact with a "man you must not miss." Some things will take a continuous relationship with that object of divine contact for God to execute His plan. That is the panorama that we will consider next. We will look at some of Jesus' disciples, who seemed to be most unlikely candidates for such a mission. We will see how God enlisted these uncouth men in the hope that His continuous contact with them would make them into the image of glory that was Heaven's blueprint when they were created.

To arrive at the place of having been made by God, some will go through painful pruning and the slashing knives of circumcision. Others will be made by means of the breaking, smashing, and firing processes on the wheel and in the kiln of the Master Potter. Whatever that process is for you, it is His desire to get you there, made into His divine image. It could be your story that is about to be told.

CHAPTER 3

He's Still at Work

A LIVING PUZZLE

The Bible is an ever-living puzzle, constantly offering a freshness so intriguing that sometimes you wonder if you have ever read it before. After teaching at a meeting some years ago, a woman walked up to me and asked to see the Bible I use. How had I pulled so much treasure from it, so many insights, she wondered. Was it the same Bible she had? I showed her my Bible and assured her that it was just the same as hers. Just the same, she told me she planned to buy herself a study Bible as soon as the meeting was over.

A few days ago, I was reading through the Gospel of John when I came across an insight in chapter 5 verse 17. I read it, paused, read it again, and went on. But even several days later, the verse would not let me go. Sensing that God might be about to reveal something to me from the verse, I returned to it. "Jesus answered them, My Father worketh hitherto, and I work" (John 5:17).

That was the response of Jesus to the legalistic Jews who had challenged Him for healing a sick and helplessly bedridden man on the Sabbath day. Actually, the man was "mat-ridden," and he had been so his entire life, some thirty-eight years. It seemed more important to those contentious Pharisees that the nest of their legalistic system remained undisturbed than that a man had been set free from the pernicious clutches of the devil. But that was not what engaged my thoughts. It was Jesus' response to the Pharisees. He said, "My Father is working *until now*" (John 5:17 NASB). *God has been working?* I pondered.

GOD'S DUTY POST

With the innocence of a child, I asked, "Father, it says in Genesis 2:2, that on the seventh day after the Creation, You rested. Why does Jesus say here that You are *still at work?*"

In my spirit, I heard these words, "No Sabbath at the moment lasts forever. (See Hebrews 4:1-11.) The Sabbath is merely one day out of seven consecutive days; it is not an eternal day. To have 'rested' on one Sabbath at the end of one week does not mean that a fresh week would not begin the following day with work resuming. Besides, the Genesis 2:2 passage you have quoted says, 'He [God] *rested*.' It does not say, 'God has been resting.' The statement was made in the past tense."

I was relieved. But that merely sparked another puzzle in my mind, so I queried further. "What work have You been doing since Your first Sabbath?"

"The world," was the response I got.

"But that is no work for the Almighty," I ventured. "All You have to do is say, 'Let there be' and everything would fall into place at once. That is not sufficient to have kept the Almighty busy *until now*, so busy that even the Psalmist remarks, 'He that keepeth thee will not slumber. Behold, he that keepeth Israel shall neither slumber nor sleep' (Ps. 121:3-4)."

The Voice said back to me, "I could have created the whole world in one day since all I had to do was say, 'Let there be.' But I didn't. I was establishing a pattern. The world I created with My words, but Man I created with My hands through a process of time and skill."

The Voice went on, "It is not the wicked in this world who keep Me busy. It is My own children. (See 2 Chronicles 7:14.) Some of them have been recalcitrant clay in My hands. If I should finish with such as these in just one 'Let-there-be' day, they would be a soggy brick. Some of the others should have been finished in one year, but instead their stubbornness against My will has taken ten years."

I was sober. Like the brooding disciples at the Passover table on the eve of the Master's betrayal, I had to ask, "Lord, is it I? Am I one of those frustrating Your calendar for their own life?"

The answer was obvious. I was one of them. The Lord then proceeded to offer a panorama of some Bible characters upon whom He had worked, just as I have been His present duty post.

THE THUNDEROUS TWO

James and John were brothers, rough fishermen toughened by their trade. They were two of the first Jesus called to be part of His team of twelve disciples. Their surname was Boanerges, which means "sons of thunder" (Mark 3:17). Not infrequently, their thunder erupted or threatened through ferocious flashes of volcanic lightning.

Jesus and His disciples approached a Samaritan village one day when suddenly, the age-old ethnic and religious bigotry between Jews and Samaritans surfaced. The Samaritans would not let Jesus' team pass through their village. At once, the brothers began to demonstrate their thunder. Of the thirteen members of the team, it was James and John who came up with an instant solution to the

Samaritan affront. Characteristically, they asked to call down fire from heaven to destroy those villagers. They reminded Jesus that Elijah himself had acted likewise. It suited them to cite the prophet Elijah in support of their wounded volatile pride. They were ready to wipe out an entire community—fathers, mothers, babies, young people, old people, immigrants, livestock—all in the name of God, and simply because the villagers refused to let them pass through their property.

Jesus had to intervene. He told them that a strange spirit had come over them. They had sought to halo their thunder by dressing it in Elijah's mantle. They had sought to use God to their selfish advantage. (See Luke 9:54-56.)

A little later, they schemed so unmindfully for the topmost positions in the fold that their very method and motive enraged the other disciples. They even hired their mother as a campaign manager to lobby Jesus. It was a family political party of two brothers and their influential and dreaded mother. The others dared not raise their voices until she was gone. In her domineering manner, she had intended to order even Jesus around when she put it bluntly to Him that her two sons should be placed on thrones to His right and to His left when His Kingdom came. She had little consideration for the other ten disciples and what they had invested into that coming Kingdom. But for the intervention of the Master, there might have been a real battle that day. (See Matthew 20:20-28.)

Even on a holy mission such as a preaching tour, those brothers would fight anyone whose doctrines or opinions differed from theirs. They flaunted their thunder shamelessly, but the Master kept working on them. (See Mark 9:38-40.) There was a treasure in them that the patient re-creative process would one day reveal.

Before the end of Jesus' three-and-a-half-year ministry, John had begun to lose his thunder. He had begun to be known as "John the beloved" and "the disciple whom Jesus loved." That's quite a change from "Thunder" to "Beloved." (See John 19:26; 20:2; 21:7,20.) He had begun to be transformed into the loving image of his Master, the One who had loved him in spite of himself. God had received him as he was, but had not left him that way.

What was the secret of this transformation from "Son of Thunder" to "Beloved"? The answer might be found partly in John 13:23,25, which says, "Now there was leaning on Jesus' bosom one of His disciples, whom Jesus loved.... He then lying on Jesus' breast saith unto Him, Lord, who is it?"

John had learned to lay his thunderous head on the Master's loving bosom, and, in the process of feeling that divine heartbeat, John had had his own head "reprogrammed." That was very unlike the story of another man, a very strong man named Samson, who lost his eyes and truncated his ministry by placing his head on a harlot's lap. (See Judges 16:19.) Where do you lay your head?

Much later, when we hear John, it is no more the voice of thunder. It is instead the tender voice of a shepherd, who often said, "Beloved, let us love one another: for love is of God; and every one that loveth is born of God, and knoweth God. He that loveth not knoweth not God; for God is love" (1 John 4:7-8).

The entire epistle of First John is a symphony of love. John had lost his thunder at the altar of the Master's breast. As for his brother James, he appears to have been no less an apostle of love. He was one of the first Christian martyrs. He was beheaded for his love for the one who had first loved him in spite of his indiscriminately volatile atomic thunders. (See Acts 12:1-2.)

It is remarkable that in their early jockeying for position, they had said "Amen" to the proposition of drinking from Jesus' cup of agony and being baptized with His peculiar baptism if it would ensure the posts for which they strove. (See Mark 10:35-40.) Accordingly,

James drank the cup of martyrdom and John was baptized, according to Church history, in a pot of boiling oil. They had said a hasty "Amen" to a prayer they never understood. What a weighty lesson that teaches us. We should never be hasty in speech, especially out of the restless passions of the flesh. It is foolish to say "Amen" to a prayer we do not understand. (See 1 Corinthians 14:16.)

THE FICKLE FISHERMAN

Peter was another strange character among the twelve. He was an impulsive extrovert, often brash. One moment he could be a channel of Jehovah asserting Jesus' divinity, and the next he could be a persuasive mouthpiece of the very devil himself. (See Matthew 16:16-17, 21-23.) None of the other disciples was known to have been so infiltrated by satan as Peter, and to have had the very devil himself (not merely some of his lieutenant demons) cast out of him. (See Matthew 16:23.)

In spite of his weaknesses, however, Peter was never to remain where he fell. That was his strength, the secret of his eventual transformation. He never hid his sins. He refused to justify his failings. He never lingered long in the mire where he fell. For instance, when the second crowing of the early morning cock jolted him into sudden realization that he had denied his Lord three consecutive times, he "went out, and wept bitterly" (Luke 22:62). He wept his way back to his Master and Maker, the One who had made him the pledge at the beginning, "Follow me and *I will make you*" (Matt. 4:19). He was determined to be made and to be made well. He contemplated no alternative to that Master, who would lovingly take him back even when he had fallen so low as to serve as an undercover agent and smooth spokesperson for the devil, their bitter foe. (See John 6:66-69.)

How very depressed Peter must have felt during the first days following his very shameful and public denial of the Master! The guilt haunted him every day and every night. The "accuser of the brethren," as the Bible calls the devil in Revelation 12:10, kept at it, whispering often into Peter's ear. The evil one was determined to convince Peter that he was unworthy, a complete disappointment as a disciple, someone who could never be made into that glorious man of God he had imagined when he first responded to the Master's invitation.

Unable to bear it any longer, one day, he seemed to have called a conference with himself. "If I cannot be made into a *fisher of men*, which was the object when I was called, then I'm going back to my nets. At least I can still be the *fisher of fishes* that I used to be." Having so concluded, he announced his desolation to the others, "*I go a fishing.*" The general reaction was a surprise. So many as six other men were ready to follow his lead and abandon the ship of discipleship. They told him right away that they were going with him.

At once Heaven was alerted. Danger loomed. Seven of Jesus' disciples were ready to abandon their calling. The resurrected Jesus paid them a visit very early the following morning. After a fruitless and disappointing night of fishing, they had not one fish to show for all their trouble. It was an unforgettable night of dismal failure that merely complicated their nagging worries.

As the disciples struggled with their fishing near shore, the Master was preparing a small fire on shore. Could He have been fanning the flames of that fire in symbolic gesture of His intent to fan the disciples back aflame? Peter and the others didn't recognize Jesus until He called out to them, asking if they'd had anything to eat. Then He told them to throw their nets on the right side of the ship, and when they did, the nets were miraculously full almost to the point of bursting. (See John 21:1-14.)

Peter must have been amazed by this turn of events. The Master had sought them out. He had chosen to prepare breakfast for a band of rebels and invite them to eat with the gravest of dissenters in their midst. Jesus told them to bring some of the fish they had just caught to place on the fire. Then He told them, "Come and dine" (John 21:12). Yes! The Master knew that He had work to do, and He could not return to His sabbath rest in Heaven until He was finished with those He had promised to "make."

More than any of the other surprises Peter received that morning on the shores of the Sea of Galilee, what followed the meal was the most unnerving act of mercy and grace. The Master invited Peter to go for a walk, during which He asked him three times, "Lovest thou me?" Each time Peter answered in the affirmative. Each response from Peter was followed with a renewal of the mandate to "Feed my lambs," and twice Peter was told to "Feed my sheep." (See John 21:15-17.)

This is the mystery I see. Peter denied His Master three times, and each denial was recorded in the file of the "accuser of the brethren," who would not see Peter beyond the point of his failures. Three times also, therefore, Peter had to state clearly his love and commitment to the Master, thus canceling out the record of those three shameful denials and receiving in exchange three fresh commissions. The whole scenario was the fulfillment of Jesus' words in Luke 22:31-32, "The Lord said, 'Simon, Simon! indeed, satan has asked for you, that he may sift you as wheat. But I have prayed for you, that your faith should not fail; and when you have returned to Me, strengthen your brethren'" (NKJV). Jesus wanted Peter to know that though he might fall, it was not going to be the end of his ministry. He was to proceed after his restoration and beyond his fall to *strengthen* his brethren who, although they might never have fallen like he, were not strong at all. If they were strong, as they might have supposed themselves to be, not having had Peter's sort of shameful experience, why would they need to be *strengthened*, and why would Peter, restored from his own disaster, become Heaven's candidate for the job? Praise God; for one fall in the dark night of his denials, Peter received three fresh mandates in the morning of his restoration. Psalm 30:5 says, "Weeping may endure for a night, but joy cometh in the morning." We may also read these encouraging words:

> *Praise be to the God and Father of our Lord Jesus Christ, the Father of mercies and the God of all comfort; Who gives us comfort in all our troubles, so that we may be able to give comfort to others who are in trouble, through the comfort with which we ourselves are comforted by God. For as we undergo more of the pain which Christ underwent, so through Christ does our comfort become greater. But if we are troubled, it is for your comfort and salvation* (2 Corinthians 1:3-6, BBE).

Beyond the darkness of Peter's perils had come the dawn of restoration as he kept in step with his loving Master along the shore of Galilee. Afterward came the Day of Pentecost, and Peter was no more the lying, swearing, fearful weakling who had denied his Master before a maid. He had been restored. He had met the Master in his morning of new creation. He had been meticulously made. He had been changed into a bold preacher for the Man he had denied, the Man who would not deny him. That was the love that changed Peter—love so strong that it kept God working on him though he was so undeserving.

Hallelujah! God blesses the penitent more than double for all their troubles! (See Isaiah 61:7.)

THE RECALCITRANT THIEF

Unlike Peter, James, and John, Judas did not submit himself to the Master's transforming purpose. Judas closed his story with suicide as a remorseful but recalcitrant thief. The same sun that melts the wax also shines on the brick that hardens. The outcome is not to be blamed on the sun but on the composition of the object on which the sun shines.

It is said of Judas that he not merely had a devil but was himself "a devil." Yet, Jesus still chose him because he represented work that was to be done. (See John 6:70-71.) Jesus was aware that Judas had a weakness for money. Jesus knew that Judas was "a thief," and yet He not only called him but entrusted him with the purse of the ministry. (See John 12:6.)

Was the assignment meant to exploit Judas' weakness? No, it was meant to heal the weakness by giving Judas an opportunity to overcome it. This is the principle used in pharmaceuticals. To immunize against yellow fever or cholera, for example, a nonlethal dose of the very disease is introduced into the body of a person. In the process of fighting the controlled dosage of the fabricated disease, the body builds up its muscles of self-defense, called "immunity." When and if the real disease presents itself, the body has been toughened enough to handle it without danger.

In Romans 5:3, we are told rather paradoxically that tribulations constitute the cure for impatience. No one would normally think of treating impatience with tribulation. But God the Creator says the escape route from every weakness is in confronting that weakness rather than avoiding it. The apostle Paul also tells us that the way to escape a temptation resides in the very temptation itself. (See 1 Corinthians 10:13.) That was why Jesus made Judas His treasurer. Perhaps that was the first time anyone had trusted Judas with money. Either way, that much trust was sufficient to challenge the thief to change his ways, especially when he knew quite well what was at stake.

Unfortunately, Judas was not a cooperative patient in God's emergency ward. He allowed himself to be lured away by his lust for money. He sold his Master for thirty pieces of silver (approximately

$600). Sadly, he never lived to enjoy the money. His obituary in Acts 1 reads in part that, although "he was numbered with us, and had obtained a part in this ministry," he pursued "the *reward* of iniquity" so recklessly that at last he "by transgression *fell*" out from the Lord's operating table. (See Acts 1:17,18,25.)

What was the reason for his fall? He kept an open window, through which the devil kept "putting" things into his heart and his life. (See John 13:2.) When his "temple" had thus been sufficiently "furnished," satan himself moved in (see John 13:27). Luke 22:3 puts it flatly, "Then entered Satan into Judas." The Gospel of John shows the *process* that led eventually to the *state* of crisis that Luke reports so bluntly.

Judas died at his own hand, disappointed by his capitulation to greed *unmade* by the Creator who had worked successfully on the others. He chose to be a hardening stone, not a melting wax. It was a pact which said, "You follow Me, I will make you. You cease following, you lose the making." When the Master gave the invitation, He was aware of the many potential distractions to the clients from His "carpentry" workshop. The invitation began a process that could be continued or terminated. Judas chose to terminate it as he turned away to catch some fleeting coins. He did not return to tell his story. It is told by his colleagues who survived the "making" process in spite of all it had taken them and the Master.

THE EX-SCARLET LADY

Preaching at a church recently, I asked the audience if anyone knew who Rahab was. Everyone remembered her as the harlot of Jericho. But that was her old identity. That was before God worked on her and she was transformed. It is surprising that the worst things about people are often better remembered than their virtues. Her change began when two men called at her brothel. She had dealt with men, all sorts of men, but these two were different. Their looks were different. Their interests were different. Their language was different. They spoke very personally and glowingly about a loving God of Heaven. Unlike the men she had known, these two were not interested in her nakedness. Something inside told her this was special. Certainly she wondered if this could be what she had longed for all those years when she sought satisfaction in sex and money. She wanted to know the God these two men served. She grabbed this unexpected opportunity firmly with both hands.

Using a scarlet rope, she let the men escape through the window of her apartment and down the city wall. Though they were fugitives, she was determined not to lose this once-in-a lifetime chance. She was prepared to face the consequences of her choice, even if it meant being prosecuted as a saboteur or for adopting an alien religion. Her determined resoluteness was her strength.

The men told her to leave the scarlet rope hanging from her window. It would serve as a sign to the returning invaders that her life and her home were to be spared. The Exodus was about to re-play itself, "When I see the blood, I will pass over you" (Exod. 12:13). That scarlet rope hanging from her window was like the scarlet blood on the doorposts of God's people on the night of the first Passover in Egypt. You can be sure she guarded that rope. It was her ticket to a new life. (See Joshua 2.)

Today her name appears in Matthew 1:5, not as Rahab, the Harlot of Jericho, but as Rachab, one of the great grandmothers of Jesus and one of only five women (four of them Gentiles) mentioned in an otherwise exclusive list of men. God had worked on her so completely that she no longer carried any trace of her reproachful past. She became so clean and holy a channel that even God's holy Son, who was God Himself, could come through it! She was made so new that it was as if she had never sinned. Not only does God change men but women as well, and He is still at work.

THE IMMIGRANT QUEEN-MOTHER

Ruth was another Gentile, a Moabite woman. The Mosaic Law said that no Moabite would be allowed into God's house until ten generations had passed. (See Deuteronomy 23:3.) But Ruth beat that law because the God of the Law was on her side. She saw her chance in her Jewish mother-in-law, Naomi, and she grabbed it. She would not procrastinate. Tomorrow was too far away. It was an uncertain future a long distance away. But she at once declared, "Thy people shall be my people, and thy God my God" (Ruth 1:16). That was her public affirmation of naturalization. She was no longer an abominable Moabitess; she was now a blessed Israelite. She became the great-grandmother of King David himself. (See Ruth 4:17.) Neither she nor her children needed to wait ten generations to enter into God's presence, as the Law demanded. God had done a quick work in her.

THE THIRSTY WOMAN BY THE WELL

There was another woman, a Samaritan, whose inner thirst kept driving her to the wells of the world, which could never satisfy her deep longings. (See John 4:4-42.) It was at one such ancestral well one hot afternoon that she met the Life Changer Himself. It appears she may have mistaken Him for a potential client, so when He asked her if she had a husband, she said that there was none, meaning to notify Him, perhaps, that she was available. But, she quickly learned that His interest in her was of another kind. She soon realized that He knew her better than she could have ever imagined. She had been seeking the passions of vain men for the water to quench the infernal thirst of her innermost soul. It was Jesus who asked her for water, but she was the one who badly needed the water only He could give her. When at last she took a drink, her transformation was so dramatic that a whole village of curious men trooped behind her to see the man who could change a notorious woman such as she.

That woman had dealt with men for a long time. She had five ex-husbands and was trying out husband number six. But in Jesus she found the Man she had always longed for—the Man who made her life worthwhile. In that Perfect Seventh she found the Life she had sought in vain in the other six. In Him she found the Water for which she had longed all her thirsty life.

So many women are lined up at the wells of the world for water that doesn't satisfy! Many have grown weary of the fanciful waters that leave them emptier than before they drank. Someone must introduce them to the Man who can give them the water of life. If only they would accept His cup but once, their hearts would sing out to be made into the women they were meant to be. If only they would.

THE YOUNG WOMAN AND THE OLD MAN

A pastor in whose church I preached last year told me the story of a young woman on the verge of suicide who walked into his office one day in much turmoil. She was a backslider. She had gone into university and joined a violent campus cult, where she had had sex with countless men and had twenty-two abortions. The pastor offered her a fresh chance to meet the Life Changer. She did. She was so transformed, she got married shortly after. Guess to whom? She married a pastor! God has a good sense of humor. Today she serves God with her husband in a mission field in Europe. She had been "made" at last by the Master she has chosen to follow. "Follow Me and I will make you" (Matt. 4:19).

The pastor told me also of a retired general in the Nigerian Army, who had repented in his old age. The old man regretted that he had wasted the better part of his seventy years seeking the Water of Life at the dry wells of some of the highest cults (or "secret societies") in the land. He wished he had known the Maker much sooner. Alas, he mourned his wasted years, the fragments of which had been rescued at last in the evening of his days!

A Sad Appointment

Recently, a pastor friend whom I had taken along on a preaching appointment told the following story. During his university days, he had met a student he felt an urge to speak to about Jesus. The urge he felt was the Creator at work, signaling that He sought an appointment with that boy, to "make" him. Strangely, the boy said that he had no time for the Gospel.

A few days later, the boy was on the roadside waiting for a taxi. He had an important appointment to keep at a party of sorts. While he waited by the sidewalk, a speeding car skidded off the road and came straight for him. Everything happened very quickly. A crash! A corpse. The boy died on the spot, a bloodied mass of flesh.

He had rejected an appointment with the Creator, while he pursued an appointment with pleasure. Sadly, his choice caused him to keep an unexpected appointment with death, unprepared, un-"made." He had no time for his Maker, but at last, somehow, he found the time to die.

And You

At Calvary, two thieves hung on crosses on either side of Jesus. They each received an invitation from Jesus to ride into Paradise with Him. One thief wasted his only chance and mocked his way into hell. The other grabbed the chance with all the common sense and strength that was left in him. He called out to Jesus, "Lord, remember me when Thou comest into Thy kingdom." Jesus wasted no time in responding to him, "Today shalt thou be with Me in paradise" (Luke 23:42-43). Had the thief hesitated, he would have missed his trip to Paradise forever.

Could a person have such a life-changing opportunity and not know it? In this case, two people had the same opportunity to be "made" by the Maker—one man took it and was saved; the other refused and was lost.

God has been at work since after His first Sabbath. He has been so busy changing lives that He neither slumbers nor sleeps. "My Father worketh hitherto, and I work" (John 5:17). Will you let Him work on you? Will you let Him change your life? Will you be wax or a stone? A John or a Judas? A Rachab or a Rahab?

> *The word which came to Jeremiah from the Lord, saying, Arise, and go down to the potter's house, and there I will cause thee to hear my words. Then I went down to the potter's house, and, behold, he wrought a work on the wheels. And the vessel that he made of clay was marred in the hand of the potter: so he made it again another vessel, as seemed good to the potter to make it. Then the word of the Lord came to me, saying, O house of Israel, cannot I do with you as this potter? saith the Lord. Behold, **as the clay is in the potter's hand**, so are ye in Mine hand, O house of Israel* (Jeremiah 18:1-6).

This is an invitation to the Potter's House. No matter how "marred" might be the clay of your life, He can make it again, yea, make you again, into "another vessel" of no less glorious design, as seems "good" to Him.

He will take you as you are, but will not leave you as you are. You should know, however, that God will not be at work forever, so He might not be awaiting you much longer. Some day soon, this world will be in its closing hours. For that reason, Isaiah solemnly pleads, "Seek ye the Lord *while* He may be found, call ye upon Him *while* He is near" (Isa. 55:6). He will not always be near; He will not always be found. Jesus Himself warned, "The night cometh when *no man* can work" (John 9:4).

How sad it would be to find yourself facing the end like one of the five foolish virgins Jesus talked to His disciples about in Matthew 25:10-12. The guests have arrived, the feast is on, and the doors are shut at last. But you find yourself outside, forever cut off from the celebration. "And the door was *shut!*"

Linger longer, if you wish, but once again be told that the time is coming—indeed, it is almost here—when "there should be time no longer" (Rev. 10:6). Pray, that you might be ready!

CHAPTER 4

The Place of New Beginnings

BEYOND DELIVERANCE

God had long made a promise that the seed of Abraham would spend a specified time in bondage before they would enter into their inheritance. (See Genesis 15:13.) The process from Egypt—the place of bondage—to the land of promise was, however, not to be an easy one. The Israelites had to pass through a place called Gilgal, a location that would have decided monumental consequences. Beyond the melodic songs of deliverance after the Red Sea; beyond the miracle of sweetened waters at Marah; beyond the manna and the quail from heaven, the nation of Israel finally arrived at Gilgal.

The rigors of the transit wilderness had been difficult to endure, but the slashing and cutting that Gilgal demanded was going to determine if that location would become a gateway into glory or a sad terminal point in the journey to the Promise. In that place, God demanded circumcision *"again."* (See Joshua 5:2.)

> *It came to pass, when all the kings of the Amorites, which were on the side of Jordan westward, and all the kings of the Canaanites, which were by the sea, heard that the Lord had dried up the waters of Jordan from before the children of Israel, until we were passed over, that their heart melted, neither was*

there spirit in them any more, because of the children of Israel. At that time the Lord said unto Joshua, Make thee sharp knives, and circumcise again the children of Israel the second time. And Joshua made him sharp knives, and circumcised the children of Israel at the hill of the foreskins. And this is the cause why Joshua did circumcise: All the people that came out of Egypt, that were males, even all the men of war, died in the wilderness by the way, after they came out of Egypt. Now all the people that came out were circumcised: but all the people that were born in the wilderness by the way as they came forth out of Egypt, them they had not circumcised. For the children of Israel walked forty years in the wilderness, till all the people that were men of war, which came out of Egypt, were consumed, because they obeyed not the voice of the Lord: unto whom the Lord sware that He would not shew them the land, which the Lord sware unto their fathers that He would give us, a land that floweth with milk and honey. And their children, whom He raised up in their stead, them Joshua circumcised: for they were uncircumcised, because they had not circumcised them by the way. And it came to pass, when they had done circumcising all the people, that they abode in their places in the camp, till they were whole. And the Lord said unto Joshua, This day have I rolled away the reproach of Egypt from off you. Wherefore the name of the place is called Gilgal unto this day. And the children of Israel encamped in Gilgal, and kept the passover on the fourteenth day of the month at even in the plains of Jericho (Joshua 5:1-10).

GILGAL

As we read in this scripture, Gilgal represents a place of fresh beginnings. Over the years, it was a place of many *firsts* for the Israelites:

1. In Gilgal, the Israelites observed their *first* Passover in the land of Promise, after decades in transit through the wilderness. (See Joshua 5:10.)

2. In Gilgal, the twelve stones of memorial from the bed of the Jordan were put down to be an eternal, *fundamental* reference point for generations yet unborn of the mercies and power of the God of Israel. (See Joshua 4:20-24.)

3. Elisha's journey into the double anointing of Elijah *began* from Gilgal and terminated beyond the Jordan, the place of the tearing apart of the veil of waters. (See 2 Kings 2:1-14.)

4. Gilgal was the place where the people were called together to "*renew* the kingdom."

5. Gilgal was where Saul was publicly anointed to *begin* his reign over Israel. Gilgal was the place where God would have put an everlasting seal on his kingship, so as to *begin* a perpetual dynasty with him, in which case there wouldn't have been the need for a David. (See 1 Samuel 11:14-15;13:4,7,13.)

6. Unfortunately, Gilgal turned out to be the place of King Saul's pathetic failure and rejection by God. There, God had meant to circumcise the last resistance in the young king's nature, so that He could begin *afresh* with him as the king forever. Unfortunately, there in Gilgal, God had to name David as a replacement to Saul—a replacement with whom He intended to *start afresh*.

> *He tarried seven days, according to the set time that Samuel had appointed: but Samuel came not to Gilgal.... And Samuel said to Saul, Thou hast done foolishly: thou hast not kept the commandment of the Lord thy God, which He commanded thee: for now would the Lord have established thy kingdom upon Israel for ever. But now thy kingdom shall not continue: the Lord hath sought Him a man after His own heart, and the Lord hath commanded him to be captain over his people, because thou hast not kept that which the Lord commanded thee. And Samuel arose, and gat him up from Gilgal* (1 Samuel 13:8,13-15).

Gilgal was also the place of convocation and sacrifice for the people of God. In other words, it was a place of personal and collective spiritual renewal. (See 1 Samuel 15:21.) Under the prophet Samuel, Gilgal also saw the *beginning* of the popular school of the prophets. (See 2 Kings 4:38.)

For the nation of Israel on their way from bondage in Egypt, Gilgal was also going to be a decisive point between the "old" from which they were fleeing and the "new" into which they were going. There, God was going to start *a new page* for them. He was going to close the old story of Egypt's *"reproach,"* which had colored all their lives, even though God's mercy and grace had been shown to them. He was going to start *a new calendar* for them, to be marked by the very significant "Happy New Year" Passover feast that they were going to hold there. So much awaited them in the future, but not before there was a sacrificial covenant of blood through the process of pain at Gilgal's circumcision slabs.

AT THAT TIME

"At that time the Lord said unto Joshua, make thee sharp knives, and circumcise again the children of Israel the second time" (Josh. 5:2).

"At that time." What time? To answer the question, we need to see the preceding verse. In verse 1, it had "come to pass," as the mighty kings of the neighboring nations heard of the incredible things God had done for His people, especially the drying up of the Jordan River, that "their courage melted away completely and they were paralyzed with fear" (Josh. 5:1 TLB).

Shouldn't that have been a right time to plant more churches, when the ovation was so loud? Shouldn't that have been a time to advance into the territory of the enemy and possess their land? No. It appears, as Paul would say, that the Spirit forbade it. (See Acts

16:6-7.) God was not going to move by their agenda. Their methods and timings were not His. As far as the Omniscient was concerned, that was the time to turn inward to His own people, not outward to the world. It was a time to prepare them to be able to properly possess the future that was surely approaching.

Alas, how often we have been deceived by the ovation! How often we have guessed the seasons of the Lord by the noises of men, rather than by the movement of His Spirit in the tops of the mulberry trees! (See 1 Chronicles 14:14-15.) Alas, how often we have fallen to our foes because, as Jesus had to lament over Jerusalem, we did not know the time of our visitation! (See Luke 19:44.)

For this great nation in transit, this time of great external ovation was not the time to advance; it was time to retreat. It was time for God to deal not with the sinners outside but with the domesticated and personalized "reproach" in His own people. The people were not going to be able to make much progress in that condition, the blinded and blinding adulations of the outsiders notwithstanding. It was time for them to lower their trousers and underpants; to open up their hidden shame to His healing knife, before the battles ahead could be guaranteed.

Circumcise Again

Why would God request the nation to be circumcised *"again"*? It was because, according to Joshua 5:4-7, this was a new generation. The generation of their fathers had been circumcised. The present generation needed its own encounter, a *fresh and personal* encounter with the knife of pain. They could no longer rest on the testimony of their long-expired fathers.

If our present generation of uncircumcised youths should be let into the Promised Land as they are, it would be a disaster. They will father prodigals and bastards with their untouched, uncircumcised tools. Already, there are many such children in our churches. Fornication, for example, is not as serious an offense after all, so long as it is done within rather than outside the church. The girlfriend or boyfriend engaged in fornication is sanctified, so long as one does not go out to her or him, but they are brought into the church. These are headed for Canaan, but their songs are the songs of Babylon. They have partaken time after time of the manna from above, but their ungrateful and insatiable appetites still crave the cucumbers of Pharaoh, their ex-tyrant. These are children who carry the badge of the God of Israel, but whose lives exhibit "the reproach of Egypt."

The other day I saw a young preacher of about twenty-five years on TV. He was sporting a conspicuously large cross on a necklace. He mixed up his scriptures and Bible characters so embarrassingly that it was clear he lacked even the basic intellectual Bible knowledge, to say nothing of the *rhema*. I could not swear that he had even been born again. I wondered if he was one of those hirelings lately coming into the fold for the gains they hope to catch. He was the pastor and founder of a church. This generation has to have its own turn at Gilgal's slashing slabs.

NO PADDED KNIVES

God was specific with Joshua about the instrument with which the circumcisions were to be done: "flint knives"; rough but sharp instruments made out of stone (sometimes iron) (Josh. 5:2 NIV). Why didn't God leave out that detail? Why didn't He choose soft rings or padded knives, which drew no blood? Why does God sometimes demand that we take the hard way before the Promised Land?

God knew what He was after—the covenant of blood, of death, of separation from the old. Any other tool would not do.

MAN BY MAN

God was after the circumcision of the whole nation, but the men had to come one by one. Corporate revival is, after all, the aggregation of individual revivals. Often, we hide in the crowd and point at the uncircumcised nature of the Church. God must start somewhere—perhaps with you, so that He might set a precedent of willing brokenness, one that others can be encouraged to follow, so that the whole land can be circumcised and a generation will be saved! Next person…You!

WHY JOSHUA?

Why did God ask the elder Joshua to do the circumcising of the majority new generation? It was because he was one of the only two surviving members of the old brigade who had themselves been circumcised. To circumcise others, he had to have been circumcised himself.

Until you have experienced something for yourself, it is just theory, regardless of how well you can narrate it. An ounce of experience is worth more than a ton of theories. You cannot give what you do not have; you cannot preach a Gospel you have never yourself received. You cannot pray holiness into the Church if you are not prepared to practice holiness yourself. It will always be necessary for the circumcised to circumcise others. The apostles could say, "That which we have *seen* and *heard* declare we unto you" (1 John 1:3). Some man might be a great orator at replaying some anointed Bishop's sermons, but the day comes when intelligent listeners begin to wonder if he bears the personal covenant seal of Gilgal beneath his beautiful pontifical cloaks.

NOT AN ANNUAL RITUAL

Circumcision is not an annual party. It is a once-and-for-a-lifetime encounter that leaves its permanent mark. When you try to dodge it, you just put off the inevitable.

Jacob did not have to have an annual wrestling match with the angel of God or keep receiving new names that marked no transformation in his life. He had one memorable encounter with the Angel of the Lord that left him limping, his hip of rebellious strength knocked out of joint. (See Genesis 32:31.) That was the mark of his "circumcision," the scar from the cutting off of his *reproachful* "Jacob" nature. Jacob meant "Deceiver," but he came out with a new name, Israel, which meant, "Prince of God." That was his license into the long-pending, promised blessing. That one circumcision carried him for life; even his children could tell of the encounter. (See Genesis 32:32.) It was a visible encounter. Everyone could see it. He did not need the tinted glasses in a church or the seraphic robes of choristers to announce it. Every step he took in life thereafter bore an unmistakable reference back to the memorable night and place of that transforming encounter.

Beyond that Gilgal, "the sun rose upon him," announcing a *new day*, a *new life*, a *new man*. He himself could thereafter declare about that place where he dislocated his thigh of self-strength, "I have seen God face to face, and my life is preserved" (Gen. 32:30).

Israel did not enter into Peniel, where "the sun rose upon him" and his life was "preserved," until his reproach had been cut off and his name had been changed from Jacob. It happened just before he crossed the brook that marked the boundary between the old from where he was coming, and the new into which he would enter. At that wrestling brook, for once, like Isaiah, he had to acknowledge his own woe. He admitted that he was Jacob, not Esau, as he had sought to convince his aged blind father two decades earlier when he stole his brother's blessing. (See Genesis 27:19-24.)

Then said I, Woe is me! for I am undone; because I am a man of unclean lips, and I dwell in the midst of a people of unclean lips: for mine eyes have seen the King, the Lord of hosts. Then flew one of the seraphims unto me, having a live coal in his hand, which he had taken with the tongs from off the altar: And he laid it upon my mouth, and said, Lo, this hath touched thy lips; and thine iniquity is taken away, and thy sin purged (Isaiah 6:5-7).

Beyond that place of God's slashing knife, Esau's sword, with that of his 400 men, waited for Jacob. He had a choice. He could dodge God's re-creative surgical knife at the brook of wrestling and face the multiple swords of Esau and his men, or he could face God and escape the merciless fury of his vengeful brother. He chose to fall before God's painful but restoring knife on this side of the brook.

Jacob sent every other person across the brook ahead of him until finally he was left alone, the only bridge into the promise apparently blocked by the God whom he had been dodging for so long. For the last time, as it were, God waited for him at the head of the bridge with the knife that would wrestle off that crooked nature from his life and replace it with the blessing that would usher him into his long-deferred prophetic destiny.

O, that God might touch us with that one indelible touch that will keep our flesh permanently out of joint but our souls in eternal covenant with Him. Gilgal is the decisive place where that will happen.

OPEN UP

Gilgal is the place where the shame that fine clothes have hidden for so long is opened up to God's surgical knife of flint. It is the place to open up our most private parts to His restoring knife. If you don't want your 'privacy' disturbed, then return to Egypt.

Before Gilgal, only the mature and discerning elders knew the secret the youths hid beneath their zealous gowns. Those boys mixed up with everyone else, and over time, everyone forgot (or ignored) their concealments. But God waited at Gilgal. There, God was going to say to them, "So far and no further." It would be time for the knives of flint.

God may tolerate the situation to a point, but the day comes when He says, "This far, and no further." Isaiah found that out. He had been a man of unclean lips, yet he was also a powerful prophet. When he encountered his Gilgal, he realized that he could go no further until he had confessed the secret he had concealed so long under his zealous proclamations of prophetic woe against other sinners. At his own Gilgal, he cried out, "Woe is me" (Isa. 6:5). Only then do we find the first record of his hearing the voice of God, the voice of commission. Isaiah was never the same after that fiery cleansing encounter.

BEYOND MANNA

The Israelites had enough reason to stop and celebrate at any of the many locations where God did spectacular things for them, in spite of their hidden reproach. They could have thrown a party at the Red Sea or built a camp at the many places where they received manna. They could have stopped to celebrate what a special breed of holy people they were, but none of those remarkable locations was their destination. A better *passage rite* experience awaited them at Gilgal, and they proceeded in that direction.

Like them, Isaiah could have gone home feeling good about having seen and heard angels, but he sought to be more than a spectator. He desired to be a participant in the glorious atmosphere he had entered. Perhaps he resolved that if his "unclean lips" were all that hindered him from that glory, he was going to open up. Out to God, therefore, he cried at once, "Woe is me, for I am undone" (Isa. 6:5).

What do you desire? Do you want an eternal encounter or just a good feeling obtained by having seen the glory and heard an angelic choir? Often, we get sidetracked by the preliminaries, short-circuited from the *best* by settling for the merely *good*. Fine clothes and good preaching may conceal certain reproaches, but they have their limits. *Gilgal.*

The time comes for each of us to open up for good if the benefits that lie beyond are to be received.

Using the *Unlikely* Man

Sometimes God will use an unlikely person to circumcise you. Joshua should have been everyone's nice and loving daddy, someone who would never cause anyone any pain. But it was he that God chose to wound them for good. To their credit, they never begrudged Joshua for it. They saw God behind the good pain and recognized that Joshua was merely His divine instrument. Often, we foolishly make enemies of those God anoints to prune us painfully into fruitfulness.

Joseph must have been greatly disappointed in his elder brothers who sold him off into slavery. For years, he carried the pain, until God showed him that their wickedness had merely been a tool in His almighty Hands. Years later, while they blamed themselves for the act, he assured them, in Genesis 45:5-8:

> *Now therefore be not grieved, nor angry with yourselves, that ye sold me hither: for God did send me before you to preserve life. For these two years hath the famine been in the land: and yet there are five years, in the which there shall neither be earing nor harvest. And God sent me before you to preserve you a posterity in the earth, and to save your lives by a great deliverance. So now it was not you that sent me hither, but God: and He hath made me a father to Pharaoh, and lord of all his house, and a ruler throughout all the land of Egypt.*

Some years later, he had to assure them again, in Genesis 50:20, "But as for you, ye thought evil against me; but God meant it unto good, to bring to pass, as it is this day, to save much people alive." God can still convert the wickedness of your brothers into His perfect purpose for your promotion, using their painful knives of stone to circumcise you into His divine image.

PAIN DEFERRED

When you try to defer the pain that comes with your initiation into divine purpose, you should know that you'll most likely have to face it again some day. Those who consistently escape the knife of Gilgal and succeed in dodging the angel at the wrestling place of transformation before the brook will surely have to confront the knives of Esau and his men beyond the brook. And that is often worse.

While those uncircumcised fellows went through the wilderness, they may have supposed that God had forgotten about their shameful concealment or that He had excused them altogether from that painful qualifying exam. But their time was coming. It had merely been deferred. The pruning you dodge today is merely deferred for another day. It must be dealt with before you receive your promotion.

PRAYERS DO NOT DELIVER THEN

Make no mistake about prayers in the season when Gilgal comes. No amount of prayer and fasting will deliver then, unless you wish to be delivered altogether from the purpose and promise that God has been leading you toward during your "forty years" in the wilderness. (See Deuteronomy 8:1-3.) Even Jesus realized that Gilgal was an inevitable bus stop. Even though He wished that the cup of agony would pass away from Him, He prayed, "not My will, but Thine, be done" (Luke 22:42-44).

What Circumcision Means

To Abraham, circumcision was a symbol of God's everlasting covenant with him and his descendents. (See Genesis 17:9-14.) The alternative to circumcision was to be "cut off" from men and from God, which meant *death*. Therefore, the men had to choose between the present pain of circumcision that would bring them into God's everlasting covenant or hindering momentary pleasures, the wages of which were death.

To Moses, circumcision was the shield from death, the gateway into life. (See Exodus 4:24-26.) To Paul, it represented the pathway to worshipping God in spirit rather than in the flesh, the key to joyful service in Christ. It was the mark of severance from the flesh and from all the things by which the flesh gloried—race, tribe, training, zeal, and all the "dung-stuff" that means so much to the uncircumcised. (See Philippians 3:3-10.)

Circumcision is the blood covenant with God, which the blood-soaked land witnesses, after which the land begins to yield to the circumcised the bumper harvests of its fruit and the gratuitous manna of yesteryear has been terminated according to God's calendar (see Joshua 5:10-12).

Jesus met His Gilgal at Gethsemane. There, cut by the knife of God's will, He bled sweat and blood, saying, "Father, not My will, but Thine, be done" (see Luke 22:41-45). Beyond that point, Calvary no longer held its terror.

The Mark of Gilgal

As the knife went to work on the young men at Gilgal, they were not laughing or having fun. They cringed, they cried, or at best they suppressed their tears. That was no place for the usual careless, lightheartedness of their uncircumcised past. It was the place of the pangs of birth.

After the knife had done its job, they did not go about with the usual proud Egyptian gait of youth. They had lost that. They walked with a strange awkwardness that defined them as just returned from God's bruising slab—very much like the limping Jacob after he met the Angel of the Lord and had his name changed to Israel, his dislocated hip the permanent mark of that memorable encounter!

That bruising season was no time for frivolity as usual. "They abode in their places" (Josh. 5:8). It was not the time to wander about trying to impress some Amalekite and Moabite girls. At last, God had their full attention.

THE MOABITES LIKED IT

Numbers 25 records how the young men of Israel went lustfully after Moabite and Midianite girls, in the process incurring the wrath of God that killed 24,000 of them in one day. (See Numbers 25:1-9.) Certainly, those heathen girls liked it the uncircumcised way. But at Gilgal, Israel was going to decide whom to please—the heathen girls or Jehovah God.

Some of us pamper our reproachful uncircumcision merely because the world hails us in those fashions that are just like theirs. We refuse the call to Gilgal, and we maintain things that God detests in our lives. We do this to please man rather than God. Because some Moabite tells us we look great in our uncircumcised fashions, we would rather displease God than dismiss their flattery. Thus we rob ourselves of the great blessings that should come to us beyond the slashing flint knives at Gilgal.

Paul declared, "I die daily" (1 Cor. 15:31). Has God succeeded in killing your flesh? Or has your carnal nature defied all sermons and all efforts by the Almighty to circumcise it? Those who dodge the knife of God will sooner fall to the knives of Esau and his merciless murderous gang.

DEALING WITH THE REPROACH

There are several reproaches, but one that God Himself calls "the reproach," that is *the reproach of Egypt.*" Similarly, there are many sins, but there is one in every person's life which the Scripture calls "the sin" that so easily besets us (see Hebrews 12:1). On the day of their circumcision, God said to the circumcised men, "This day have I rolled away *the reproach* of Egypt from off you" (Josh. 5:9).

The implications are frightful. If God was only then rolling back the reproach from off them, that would mean they had been carrying it all the while they were enjoying the miracles of the manna and the crossing of the Jordan River. They had a reproach—one that God Himself recognized—and yet they still had access to the miracle waters that flowed from the rock, the sweetened waters of Marah, and the daily rations of manna that the Lord sent down from on high.

Sometimes we misinterpret the many favors God graciously bestows on us to mean that we have no case with Him at all. We ask ourselves why He would otherwise grant us such an abundant supply of manna. Why would He open the Jordan River for us? Why should the rocks issue water in response to our need? Meanwhile, we fail to notice how many thousand deaths we have endured while we seemed to have been enjoying those merciful favors.

The generous hand of God is not always a measure of His heart. His gifts are not always a sign that He is pleased with our ways. The mercy of God is not a measure of our righteousness. God's gracious sunshine and rainfall do not always demonstrate how He distinguishes the just from the unjust. (See Matthew 5:45.)

The people of whom we now speak had left Egypt, but Egypt had not left them. They were a people blessed of God but tainted with the stigma of Egypt. They ate heavenly manna while they were yet uncircumcised outsiders to the Abrahamic covenant with Jehovah.

THE FRUIT OF THE LAND

A number of benefits resulted from the process at Gilgal. Mighty Jericho became almost a walkover, and the land began to yield its treasures to the new nation of circumcised people.

Before the circumcision, it had been a nation of adult babies who had to be "manna-fed" daily. They were never to know, while they celebrated that spoon feeding, that the land was ready to yield to them its fruit if they would grow into circumcised men through the demands of the testing slabs of Gilgal.

The children of Israel encamped in Gilgal, and kept the Passover. ... And they did eat of the old corn of the land on the morrow after the passover unleavened cakes, and parched [roast] corn in the selfsame day. And the manna ceased on the morrow after they had eaten of the old corn of the land; neither had the children of Israel manna any more; but they did eat of the fruit of the land of Canaan that year (Joshua 5:10-12).

Until God stops our manna of grace, some of us will never know anything more than the merciful rations upon which we have depended all our uncircumcised lives in the wilderness. God desires to reveal deeper things to us, but not until we have gone through the knives at Gilgal and the manna we received as babies has ceased.

The manna should cease when we have become grown men who work the land, harvesting a variety of crops rather than depending daily on the changeless menu that comes from Heaven without our effort or input. Until then, we do not graduate into givers. We will remain grateful receivers. Nobody gathered manna primarily to give out of it to others. There was a measured ration for each family. (See Exodus 16:16-18.) Each person consumed their ration, and God never made a case with anyone because they did not pay a tithe out of their manna. The demands of tithe and the overflows of harvest were the portion of the generations beyond the wilderness, that sowed and thereafter enjoyed the blessings of "the fruits of the land." There was no need to share the manna; each person had a specific portion. Like little babies guarding their candies, we who have nothing but manna are unable to give freely.

In our narrow ministries, limited businesses, confined and harassed families, and our manna-dependent spiritual lives, there is so much fruit of the land of Canaan that is waiting to be discovered. But to obtain it, we must submit to the God-ordained, pain-inflicting knives at Gilgal, and God must pull the routine manna from our menus.

Manna is an un-worked-for gracious supply of daily sustenance, whereas the fruit of the land is the reward of labor that comes with variety. Manna is good, but the fruit of the land is better. Manna is from God, so also is the yield of the land. However, the land will not yield to the uncircumcised, whose blood has been too delicate to stain the earth with its signature of a covenant with God.

I pray that God will stop the flow of easy manna to someone today, that they may begin to till the ground and enjoy the bounty of the fruit of the land.

HAPPY NEW YEAR

Beyond the knives, God opened a *new* page to the *new* nation. The reproach of Egypt had been rolled away. A new day, a new page, a new history had begun. That was the significance of the Passover they celebrated at that imperative bus stop of Gilgal, for the Passover marked a happy New Year in the Jewish calendar. It marked the day the Israelites came "out of Egypt, out of the house of bondage." It was to them "the beginning of months" and "the first month of the year" (Exod. 12:2).

The bruising of Christ's flesh was like the opening of the gateway for the release of His spirit into the glorious presence of God. It was only after His flesh had been bruised that He could pray, "Father, into Thy hands I commend My spirit" (Luke 23:46). Like Christ, the slashing away of their flesh by circumcision opened a gateway for those ex-slaves from reproach to bounty.

Is there something in you that is hindering you from entering into and enjoying the land into which God is taking you? I pray that He will lead you this day through Gilgal, by choice or by force. I pray that the new man would begin to arise and live in you as you let God, by whatever knives He chooses, slash away that uncircumcised badge of Egypt that has become a delicate, private part of your old person. I pray His merciful knife will this day locate that private *reproach* you have meticulously concealed from public view and defended with every shield of garments your efforts can afford. Beyond Gilgal, may the Lord grant you a Passover, a *new page*. May He then cut off the manna upon which you have depended for so long. It is time for the land to yield unto you its freshness, its abundance, yea, "the fruit of the land of Canaan."

CHAPTER 5

Broken for Service

THE MANY WITNESSES

Have you ever sung the song:

Have Thine own way, Lord! Have Thine own way!
Thou art the Potter, I am the clay.
Mold me and make me after Thy will,
While I am waiting, yielded and still.
(Adelaide Pollard, 1907)

If you have, then you have prayed a good prayer. There are those whose training will be solely from following the Maker. Others, God will "make" only by breaking them. After all, it has been said that some will never look up until God lays them on their backs. There are different therapies for different maladies.

On three occasions in the Bible, God took time to show the process of breaking that His people would undergo before He could send them forth to save a dying world. Those three witnesses are concealed in the two instances when Jesus multiplied bread to feed several thousand hungry followers and the one occasion at the Last Supper when He broke the Passover bread. "In the mouth of two or three witnesses shall every word be established" (2 Cor. 13:1; Matt. 18:16).

MESSIANIC TYPES

In the Scriptures, Jesus is described in terms of various symbols or types. He is the *Bread of Life*, the *Water of Life* or *Living Water*, and the *Lamb of God*, for example. (See John 6:35,48,51; John 4:14; 7:38; 6:35; John 1:29.) Whatever Jesus is, we are also. That is why we are called "Christians," which means "Little Christs." For instance, Jesus says in John 8:12 that He is "the light of the world," and declares in Matthew 5:14 that we are also "the light of the world." We read in 1 John 4:16 that "God is love." The eighth verse of the same chapter states that we who identify with Him ought also to partake of the same nature. Little wonder that *God*, our Heavenly Father, says we, His children, are also *gods*. (See Psalm 82:6; John 10:34.).

In John 6, verses 35 and 48, Jesus describes Himself using the symbol of bread when He says, "I am the bread of life." Through the miracles of the feeding of the five thousand and later, the four thousand, Jesus, as we shall soon see, sought to demonstrate to the disciples that they were bread of life just as He was the Bread of Life. (See Mark 6:30-44; 8:1-13.) The mystery foreshadowed in those miracles had to be later stressed by means of the Last Supper, during which there was another breaking of bread.

At the Last Supper, Jesus showed Himself as the Bread broken for us when He broke the communion bread and said of it, "This is my body" (Matt. 26:26). When Jesus miraculously multiplied the bread and the fish to feed His hungry followers, He demonstrated that His followers should also be broken bread for their hungry, fainting generation. How do we know? At the Last Supper, Jesus broke the bread (which He said was His body) for the disciples to eat. When He multiplied the bread and fish, He instructed the disciples to take the broken bread to the people. This was symbolic of how they needed to be *broken* so that the multitude would be fed and thereby saved from fainting from hunger on their way home. (See Mark 8:6.) The Lord's Supper demonstrates *God's* sacrifice for us, but the miracles of bread and fish demonstrate what ought to be *our* sacrifice for the sake of a threatened world.

Of the bread that Jesus broke at the Last Supper, He said, "This is my body which is *given* for you" (Luke 22:19). In 1 Corinthians 11:24, Jesus says, "this is My body, which is *broken* for you." The two passages together convey the following idea, "My body which is *given* for you and *broken* for you."

If that bread that Jesus used at that first communion service represented His body, then the processes through which the bread went were supposed to be prophetic pointers to the processes through which His sacrificial flesh was to go in the course of the redemption of humanity. Accordingly, the breaking of that bread had to have been symbolic of the breaking of His body. In addition, the Bible states that we are the Body of Christ, each individual Christian being a member (a part) of that Body, with Christ being the Head. (See 1 Corinthians 12:27; Romans 12:4-5; Ephesians 1:22-23.) It follows, therefore, that what Jesus did during that Last Supper was also intended to refer ultimately to *us*, the members of His Body, of which He is the Head. By partaking of the Lord's Supper (the Holy Communion), we identify with the Lord Himself and show ourselves willing to be continually broken as He was.

RECURRING PATTERNS

When Jesus took up the bread at the Last Supper, He did something to the bread before making it available to the disciples. He *broke* it. Altogether, the bread went through *three* stages before He gave it to the disciples. It is all there in Matthew 26:26: "As they were eating, Jesus took bread, and blessed it, and brake it, and gave it to the disciples, and said, Take, eat; this is My body."

First, He *took* the bread; next, He *blessed* the bread; and finally, He *broke* the bread. It was only after those initial steps that He *gave out* the bread to the disciples, asking them to eat it. He did not send the bread out on its mission before it had gone through those three processes.

On the two occasions when bread was multiplied for the feeding of the multitudes, the same pattern was followed. First, at the feeding of the five thousand, we read, "When He [Jesus] had *taken* the five loaves and the two fishes, He looked up to heaven, and *blessed*, and *brake* the loaves, and *gave* them to his disciples to set before them [the multitude]" (Mark 6:41).

Next, at the feeding of the four thousand we read, "He *took* the seven loaves, and *gave thanks*, and *brake*, and *gave* to His disciples to set before them [the multitude]" (Mark 8:6).

The process consisted of taking, blessing (praying over the bread), breaking, and finally serving the broken bread. Could it be a coincidence that the same pattern was meticulously repeated on three different occasions? Certainly, there was a significant reason for it, and the three different "witnesses" were intended to stress that significance.

THE SAVED AND SANCTIFIED BREAD

If we accept that the bread in each case was symbolic, as Jesus said of the Passover bread, then the first act of *taking* the bread seems to symbolize, to me, the first necessary and significant spiritual act of coming to Christ. This would be the preliminary act of salvation by which we hand our lives over to Him as Savior, and He takes us for His own, becoming our Master, to do with us as He pleases. Before this willing act of surrender, we belonged to a different master. But once Christ has taken us as His own, we become His property, committed into His hands.

The second step of *blessing* the bread signifies the sanctification, the consecration, and the setting apart for God's holy purpose of the believer. The Bible states in 1 Timothy 4:5 that the prayer of thanksgiving we make over what we eat *sanctifies* the food. We may say, therefore, that something more, a further spiritual element of sanctification or separation unto God, was added to the bread— the believer—by the prayer of thanksgiving that was made over it.

Did the Lord end there with the bread? No. He could not send out that bread yet, although it had been, as it were, both *saved* and *sanctified*. He could not commission it with the mandate to save that famishing generation, until He had also *broken* it.

BEYOND SALVATION AND SANCTIFICATION

Like that bread, we are of little use to our generation until we are broken. Brokenness is a further stage from salvation. Beyond salvation, beyond sanctification, there has to be a breaking. The bread could not be commissioned to save the multitude until it had been broken. In the same way, God cannot make much use of the person who is not broken, even though that person may have been "saved and sanctified," as we would usually say.

THE SIGNIFICANCE OF THIS BREAD

Whatever Jesus is, we also are, in a way. He is Light, and so are we. He is Love, and so are we. He is Bread; so also are we. At the Last Supper, Jesus provided the bread He served to His disciples, saying it was His body. Even though the disciples had been involved in arranging the venue for that occasion, there is no record that He asked them to provide the bread, as He had done when He fed the crowds. On that night with His disciples, the bread emanated from Him and was broken by Him. (See Luke 22:8-20.) The

Bible says that when the hour came, He simply broke the bread. When He fed the thousands, however, He asked His *disciples* to make the bread available. That was because the bread in that case was going to be symbolic of the disciples being broken for service. He said to them, "Give ye them to eat" (Mark 6:37). In other words, "You should give them to eat. *You* should provide, break, and serve *this* bread because it is going to symbolize something that concerns you."

Unfortunately, the disciples tried to pass the responsibility off to the multitude. They advised Jesus to send the people away, so that they could be responsible for feeding themselves. The disciples gave all sorts of excuses why *they* could not provide the bread. That unwillingness to make sacrifices or be inconvenienced for the welfare of the people only showed how unbroken they were and the vital necessity of the process the Master was about to institute. They said that the place was far away and it was too late in the evening. Besides, they had computed the cost of feeding that crowd to be equivalent to a whole year's wages. Who could afford such a cost, they wondered.

Eventually, the bread was made available to Jesus *by the disciples.* He received it from *their* hands, although it had emanated from the multitude. In that way, the two groups were both taking part in the symbolic miracle He was going to perform. Both the disciples and the multitude fulfilled their mutual roles. The bread was going to symbolize how broken one group should be in the hands of the Master before it could minister to the other larger group. After the Master had performed His role concerning the loaves, He broke them and gave them to those whom the loaves represented, the disciples. The disciples in turn broke them and served them to the multitude. At the Last Supper, He did not need anyone else to further break the bread after He had broken it. He simply broke it and served it. When He fed the multitudes, however, He broke the bread and then handed the broken loaves over to the disciples who further broke the loaves before serving the crowd.

BY THE MOUTH OF TWO

The Bible says that by the mouth of two or three witnesses, *every truth* would be established. (See 2 Corinthians 13:1.) The repetition of this miracle of multiplication of bread was for establishing a truth. It would appear that the disciples had failed to grasp the significance of the miracle in the first instance, hence the need to repeat it a second time with a different number of loaves and a different number of fishes for a different number of people. Meanwhile the key players remained unchanged—the disciples and the Master. The pattern or processes through which the bread went also remained basically the same on both occasions. The disciples made the loaves of bread available and delivered the loaves to the Master with their own hands, then Jesus:

1) *took* the bread

2) *blessed* the bread

3) *broke* the bread

4) and *gave* the broken loaves to the disciples, who were to further break and serve the bread to their respective allotments of hungry congregations of fifties and hundreds, who were on the verge of fainting from hunger. (See Mark 8:1-9.)

This was repetition for emphasis. "The word of the Lord came unto Jonah the *second* time" (Jon. 3:1). To us, it has come a third time.

BROKENNESS BEFORE SERVICE

Often, we pray, "God, use me; God, use me," yet God does not respond to our frantic pleas because He knows He cannot use us until we have been broken. Truly, there is a great need out there in the form of a waiting hungry multitude. The Master Himself is with us, desiring to help those into whose lives He has already invested much. Only one thing stands between the Master and the multitude, the broken bread.

The fact that there is an urgent need in the form of a hungry multitude does not mean that God will step away from His pattern. He will wait until there is bread to be broken.

THE PAINFUL SIDE OF THE BREAKING PROCESS

After the prayer of sanctification over the bread, Jesus broke the bread and then passed the pieces to His twelve disciples. Having received the pieces of bread from their Master, the disciples broke the bread again into smaller pieces and served the multitude. The breaking was, therefore, a continuous process begun first by the Lord and continued by His disciples.

The breaking process may originate from God Himself, but He will further use other instruments to perfect it. Sometimes the breaking is more painful because of the persons or instruments involved. We are ready to bear the pain when those who break us are those we know as enemies. But when God uses His disciples as instruments in the process of breaking us, it becomes unbearably painful because they are friends or brothers and sisters in the Lord. Think about how Caesar felt when Brutus, his friend, stabbed him in Shakespeare's *Julius Caesar,* or Jesus when He was betrayed by Judas, His friend. (See Matthew 26:50.) Regardless of the vessel God uses, we can choose to see God in the process and respond like Joseph did when he said, "Fear not: for am I in the place of God? But as for you, ye thought evil against me; but God meant it unto good, to bring to pass, as it is this day, to save much people alive" (Gen. 50:19-20).

WRONG RESPONSES TO GOD'S FORMATION

Because breaking is generally painful, people react in various ways when confronted with it. Where we, the *bread*, are unable to see

God at work, the usual thing would be for us to complain, grumble, and murmur against the Lord, the wicked disciples, and the multitude that has taken sides against us. For this very reason, some have fled the process. They did not want to lose their *breadness* or submit to being ruffled, maltreated, or broken. Some fought with the agents God had raised up to break them. They answered saying, "Must you talk to me like that? Am I your equal? Is Christianity an excuse for you to treat me this way? I'll show you that you are nobody!" They bragged and fought and boasted and lost what God had meant to achieve in their lives. The self in them was unwilling to die.

More Broken than Others

On both occasions when the bread was multiplied, Jesus broke the loaves of bread and then handed the broken pieces to His disciples. On the first occasion, when He fed 5,000 men and an unknown number of women and children, Jesus began with five loaves. (See Mark 6:30-44.) If there had been six loaves, then we could assume, perhaps, that each loaf was initially broken once into two halves, one half for each of the twelve disciples. But there were only five loaves. Each loaf broken only once would mean there was enough for only ten of the disciples. Two of the halves would have had to be broken again. Those two half loaves broken twice would represent those who are chosen or called to serve more people or prepared for a higher service.

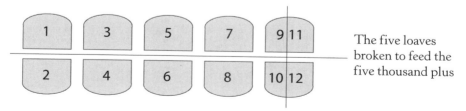

The five loaves broken to feed the five thousand plus

On the second occasion when seven loaves of bread were multiplied to feed 4,000 men plus an unspecified number of women and children, a similar thing may have happened. Some loaves may have been broken less often than others. This is why no loaf should compare itself with another loaf. Some loaves will of necessity be broken more often and into smaller fragments than others because they have a greater work to do. No loaf should, therefore, complain and say, "O Lord, that fellow over there is bread like I am. We were baked in the same oven, the same day. He does not have to go through all this. Why must I?"

STAGES OF BROKENNESS

Paul was speaking of the same experience of continuous breaking when he said, *"I die daily"* (1 Cor. 15:31). We see a type of this at the feeding of the multitudes. *First*, the Lord broke the loaves of bread and handed a portion to each disciple. Second, each disciple broke his bread again as he served groups of fifty to one hundred. Third, each individual who received a twice-broken piece of bread from the disciples broke it into smaller pieces that could be easily eaten. The breaking agents in all three initial stages, therefore, were generally the *hands*.

At this third stage of breaking, the bread still maintained its nature; the work was not complete. Therefore, the bread had to pass through another process. It was broken a *fourth* time as it was chewed in the mouth. In the mouth, the bread encountered one of the most painful stages of the breaking process. It was broken up and pounded upon and smashed and crushed and mashed and smashed again and again. The *teeth*, the breaking agents at work at this stage, served as powerful hammers crushing the bread into tiny bits. This represents a terrible breaking experience. At this stage, the bread loses its nature, its beautiful *breadness*.

Apart from the teeth, which break the *body* of the bread into bits, alkaline agents in the saliva are also at work on the inner properties or *soul* of the bread in the mouth. This breaks it into a form that can be received by the human body. The work of the enzymes in the saliva represents the *fifth* stage of breaking for the bread.

Regardless of how painful the breaking process has been to this point, the breaking process is not yet over because the body still cannot absorb the bread in its present state. For that reason, the bread is moved down into the stomach, *separated* even farther from the outside world. It moves out of reach into the warm darkness and confinement of the stomach. It is there, alone, that it encounters the agonies of the last stages of the breaking process.

The *sixth* stage of the breaking process takes place in the *stomach*. The agents are chemicals that deal not just with the bread but with something in the bread—the germs that may have hidden in the bread and survived in it up until that point, unseen by the unaided physical eyes. These germs have followed the bread so long that they have become part of the bread's nature. They might also be thought of as a remnant of the sin nature in the bread. These germs must be cast off and destroyed because they are dangerous to the body. Beyond the *body* of the bread, these chemical agents in the stomach act on the *spirit* of the bread to give it a new, free nature. Only after that does the bread (still carbohydrate in form) proceed into the *small intestines* where the *seventh* and final breaking process takes place before the bread is absorbed by the body.

Shouldn't the bread, now in the prison house of the intestines, finally have some rest from trouble? No. Our knowledge of body chemistry tells us that there are still other powerful and sometimes very acidic agents that continue to *minister* to the bread. These totally change the nature of the bread into something very simple, very different, very new. Acted upon at this *seventh* stage in the process of digestion in the small intestines, the bread is broken down finally into what is known as "simple sugar," the only state in which the bread can be absorbed by the body into the blood stream (or *life stream*, because blood *is* life). (See Leviticus 17:14.)

At this stage, the bread's "outer man" releases its "inner man" (or inner powers), sending latent energy into the body, providing life and vitality. By the time the "carcass" of that broken bread exits the body, it should have been able to say, "I have fought a good fight, I have finished my course, I have kept the faith" (2 Timothy 4:7).

What is the seventh stage for the majority of broken loaves, however, will be the *eighth* stage for those who had initially been broken more than once. Once more, a summary of the stages:

1. Jesus breaks the bread to give to His disciples.

2. The disciples break the bread to give to the multitude.

3. Each person in the multitude breaks the bread to put into their mouth.

4. The *body* of the bread in the mouth is completely broken down and chewed by the teeth.

5. Enzymes in the mouth break the *soul* of the bread and pass it down to the stomach.

6. Chemicals in the stomach deal with remnant germs in the bread and pass the mashed bread further down into the small intestines.

7. Chemical agents in the small intestines further break the *body* of the bread to release the *spirit* of the bread. That *spirit* is the simple sugar into which the carbohydrate was converted. This transformed bread, as simple sugar, energizes the body as it is absorbed through the walls of the small intestines.

8. For the loaves that had initially been broken more than once, what represents a seventh stage would have been to them the "extra mile" of an eighth stage.

SIMPLE SUGAR

The body cannot make use of food or derive energy from it until it is broken down to this simple form. If you were to insert even a very small piece of unbroken-down bread into the blood stream, it would cause death. Similarly, the Body of Christ cannot absorb us and we cannot provide energy or life to it until we have been broken down to our *simplest* form. This may be why the unbroken ones have often caused the Body of Christ (and the members thereof) so much death and so much trouble.

When the Lord starts to break us, we may pass through several stages and several "breaking agents." Some of these breaking agents may be disciples of the Lord or some great man of God. A further stage may involve other agents, members of the congregation of the Lord. Sometimes the disciples finish with us only to pass us on to the people, the public, the multitude, who bite us apart, tear us down to nothing, and pass us on still to other more corrosive agents, until nothing is left of us. We have been changed into everything we are in Christ—someone with a new nature, a heavenly nature, a simple, sweet nature.

For you to be continuously useful, you have to be continuously broken. You stop being useful when you stop being broken, or stop "dying daily."

BROKEN TO THE LEAST

Each stage of the breaking process reduces the previous piece into smaller bits, but it does not annihilate the bread. God will break you down to your least unit, even your cell unit. He will keep breaking you until every evil tendency is dealt with. Your tongue will be broken, if not in the second stage, maybe in the fourth. Your nature will be broken, your appetite will be broken, your temper will be broken. God will go on breaking you smaller and smaller, until you are lost in Him, but only if you will surrender to Him. He will go on breaking you so that you can be given to your waiting hungry generation that is about to faint. Will you show up quickly, ready to do the first thing: surrender yourself completely and willingly to Him? He cannot break bread that He has not received.

CONSTANTLY BROKEN, BUT ALWAYS FULL

Does it not amaze you that the little piece of bread Jesus broke and placed into the hands of the disciples was able to feed the entire section of the crowd that disciple had to serve? There is no way the little piece of bread that each disciple had in his hands could have fed even two hungry men, unless the bread was constantly multiplying in the hands of the disciple. As a disciple broke from the bread in his hand to serve someone, what was left grew back to the previous size (or even bigger). The natural thing would have been for the bread to dwindle as more and more pieces were taken from it. But the *supernatural* happened and the bread grew instead of dwindling.

Jesus made the same point in John 12:24, when He stated that unless a grain of corn falls into the ground and dies, it won't multiply. It can't minister food to people and will abide alone until it ultimately dies and is wasted. In other words, the grain of corn is propagated, not exterminated, by the breaking process of *germination* peculiar to corn, which Jesus described as a kind of death. This is significant. The breaking process does not reduce you. It increases you and multiplies your usefulness.

THE TOTAL MINISTRY OF THE BROKEN BREAD

In its finest and final form as simple sugar, the bread is able to minister to the whole body, not merely part of the body. The eyes, legs, hands, and head all receive strength from the fully broken bread, which is carried as simple sugar in the blood stream and flows into the vessels that are channeled through those parts. Unbroken bread might please the eyes with its shape. It might minister to the nose with its promise of sweetness and fine aroma. In the mouth, it certainly will minister sweetness to the taste buds. But in the blood vessels, as simple sugar, it provides energy to the whole body.

Your most broken form is the form in which you are most useful to everyone, not just to some. The unbroken preacher may minister to the eyes with his or her fantastic dressing, and to the ears with his or her good voice and thrilling rhetoric. But only broken bread can minister to the whole body, to the deep needs of the belly, and thereafter to the legs, hands, bones, and blood.

Have you wondered why your usefulness is limited to only part of the Body of Christ? The answer may be found in your unwillingness to be completely broken.

Often, we run from the breaking process because we fear it will take something out of us, reduce us, humble us, and bring us to the level of the commoner. That is what the world thinks. God states, on the other hand, that the way to be master is to first be a servant, and the way to be exalted is to be humble. (See Mark 9:35; 10:44-45 and James 4:6,10; Luke 14:11.) No seed multiplies before it has died. The way to increase is to be broken. Until the bread was broken, it could not increase in the hands of the disciples.

The breaking process will not reduce you, it will only increase you, and multiply how many ways you may be useful to your generation—the waiting hungry multitude. There is no limit to the multitude that any bread can feed if it is sufficiently broken.

THE BREAD THAT WON'T BE BROKEN

There will always be some bread that refuses to be broken. It is determined to maintain its beautiful shape. It will never allow its colorful dress of a wrapping bag to be taken off, because it perceives it to be too much of a demotion. Always and in every place where this bread has the chance to show off, it proudly displays the label of the prestigious bakery of its origin and ancestry. Proudly it announces to other loaves, "I am no commoner bread like you are. I was not baked by just any baker." Proudly it carries itself high above all others. It will give nothing up—not its dress, its business-card billboard that bears its fanciful name, or its shape, or its fine smell. It will give up nothing for the breaking process. Thus it remains intact—elegant but useless.

What will happen to this fashionable, decorative bread that no one may touch, let alone eat? It will remain beautiful, but only for a while. Bread is made to be eaten, not for show. After a few days, if it is not eaten, it will become moldy. A bread disease attacks it and fungus settles on it. It will die the death of all unbroken bread. Its wonderful wrapper or the label of that prestigious wonderland where it was made will not be able to defend it against the fungal invasion. Soon its beauty is replaced with repulsive ugly rottenness. At that point, no one will care about its colorful dress or the long and prestigious list of its ingredients. No one will care where it was baked or by whom. It has expired. It will be picked up by a gloved hand, taken out of the house, placed in a trashcan casket, and then thrown into a rubbish dump cemetery to be feasted upon by scavenger dogs, vultures, and maggots. The bread has been broken at last, but too late to be useful for anything. Had it allowed itself to be broken, it would still have been alive in its converted form as simple sugar providing energy for the body in which it is serving.

That will be the fate of those who won't be broken. Their usefulness will soon expire. They will die invaded by the sickness of bread. They will lose their sweet aroma and beauty to an invading fungus. Men will cast them out. Their place hereafter will be among the refused, the worthless, the useless, the wasted, the rotten, and the dead—a kind of hell. Either way, the bread will be broken, whether by the Master or by the fungus and maggots of death.

You have a choice. The Master has need of you, to meet the needs of a waiting, hungry, vast humanity. Either the Lord breaks you and uses you, or the fungus will soon overwhelm you, making you good for nothing; salt without savor, to be thrown out and trodden under the feet of men. (See Matt. 5:13.)

Sinners are also a kind of rotten bread. Jesus will judge all those who are rotten bread unless they repent. He won't serve any bread to His precious people unless He has first, *taken* it, *blessed* it, and *broken* it.

WHERE IS THE BREAD?

The multitude is waiting, and the Master also—His hands are stretched out to receive you, bless you, break you, and serve you to this hungry, fainting generation. The multitude is seated, waiting for bread in expectant companies of fifties and hundreds. The Master still waits as well. But where is the bread? Mark 6:34-44 says:

Jesus, when He came out, saw much people, and was moved with compassion toward them, because they were as sheep not having a shepherd: and He began to teach them many things. And when the day was now far spent, His disciples came unto Him, and said, This is a desert place, and now the time is far passed: Send them away, that they may go into the country round about, and into the villages, and buy themselves bread: for they have nothing to eat. He answered and said unto them, Give ye them to eat. And they say unto Him, Shall we go and buy two hundred pennyworth of bread, and give them to eat? He saith unto them, How many loaves have ye? go and see. And when they knew, they say, Five, and two fishes. And He commanded them to make all sit down by companies upon the green grass. And they sat down in ranks, by hundreds and fifties. And when He had taken the five loaves and the two fishes, He looked up to heaven, and blessed, and brake the loaves, and gave them to his disciples to set before them; and the two fishes divided he among them all. And they did all eat, and were filled. And they took up twelve baskets full of the fragments, and of the fishes. And they that did eat of the loaves were about five thousand men [besides women and children].

Then in Mark 8:1-9, we read:

In those days the multitude being very great, and having nothing to eat, Jesus called his disciples unto Him, and saith unto them, I have compassion on the multitude, because they have now been with me three days, and have nothing to eat: And if I send them away fasting to their own houses, they will faint by the way: for divers of them came from far. And His disciples answered Him, From whence can a man satisfy these men with bread here in the wilderness? And He asked them, How many loaves have ye? And they said, Seven. And He commanded the people to sit down on the ground: and He took the seven loaves, and gave thanks, and brake, and gave to His disciples to set before them; and they did set them before the people. And they had a few small fishes: and He blessed, and commanded to set them also before them. So they did eat, and were filled: and they took up of the broken meat that was left seven baskets. And they that had eaten were about four thousand: and He sent them away.

THE RELEASE OF ENERGY

Energy is merely potential in the bread; it is not released until the bread is broken to its last form. The point of the final breaking is the point of the release of energy—latent energy. Energy is present in the bread, but it is imprisoned. The breaking releases the energy that otherwise would not have been of any use to anyone. Alas, how many unbroken loaves have died unfulfilled with what they carried but never gave!

The same bread which gives life when broken fully may also cause harm if not broken properly. For instance, if not broken, bread can choke and kill. If not broken appropriately, it can cause constipation. If fully broken, the same bread will energize. The difference between ministering life or death seems to lie in the brokenness of the bread.

This situation can be seen in the Body of Christ today. There are many with great potential. They smell fine, taste fine, look well baked and well dressed. They have an impressive curriculum vitae of who they are and all the important places where they have been. But you can't take them into the holiest place. They minister death. Their preaching is wonderful, but their lives are in terrible condition. They minister very well to the nose and the eyes and the taste buds, but beyond that, they are dangerous. They preach well enough to tickle our ears. They sing well enough to delight us. They may even pray many hours a day, but they have not been chewed and smashed. They love their delicate, sophisticated, and civilized exterior too much to lose it to the breaking process. Their usefulness is limited. They do not minister *energy*, despite the great promises they hold.

THE BENEFITS OF BROKENNESS

John 12 has two different but related and valid references to the benefits of brokenness. First, in verses 3-7 we read about the breaking of the alabaster box of pure and precious oil:

> *Then took Mary a pound of ointment of spikenard, very costly, and anointed the feet of Jesus, and wiped His feet with her hair: and the house was filled with the odour of the ointment. Then saith one of his disciples, Judas Iscariot, Simon's son, which should betray him, Why was not this ointment sold for three hundred pence, and given to the poor? This said he, not that he cared for the poor; but because he was a thief, and had the bag, and bare what was put therein. Then said Jesus, let her alone.*

Until the box or bottle of the perfume was broken, there was no release of sweetness into the air. This account in John does not seem to mention a breaking. But the account in Mark 14:3-4 does, "She *brake* the box, and poured it on his head." It was "an alabaster box of ointment of spikenard *very precious.*" Before the breaking, some other power, maybe a foul power, held sway over the air. Or maybe it was simply the usual stale air as it had always been "in the beginning, is now, and ever shall be." Whatever it was, there was a release after the breaking. It was a very painful breaking for the oil was "very costly."

Some of Jesus' disciples felt her painful sacrifice was a foolish waste. The account in Mark 14:4 states that it was not just one person who felt that way. That is what you should expect when the breaking begins—public criticism and ridicule, sometimes even from other Christians.

We can perfume this stinking world if we are willing to be broken. It says in Second Corinthians 2:14 that, as Christ's *captives* (those He has taken, blessed and broken), we are a fragrance for God in every place.

The second reference to brokenness, found in John 12:23-25, says:

> *Jesus answered them, saying, The hour is come, that the Son of man should be glorified. Verily, verily I say unto you, Except a corn of wheat fall into the ground and die, it abideth alone: but if it die, it bringeth forth much fruit. He that loveth his life shall lose it; and he that hateth his life in this world shall keep it unto life eternal.*

It says here that the time came for Jesus to be glorified, but not before there was a dying of the grain. In other words, death becomes necessary when the time comes to be glorified. The grain of corn that should be glorified falls into the ground and is *broken* through a process that we would usually refer to as germination, but which Jesus refers to as *death*. Through this breaking, the corn loses its identity. It ceases to live. It rots. It dies. It is lost. Then it receives a new life, a new nature, as it begins to respond upwards to the sunlight from above. Now it climbs higher and higher, after previously falling down and dying. Then it ministers fresh life to several other grains. It has been fruitful in dying.

Brokenness, one might dare to say, is a vital key to any kind of successful Christian living. The broken disciple is a sweet fragrance for God in a rotten world. Brokenness brings sweetness where we have often known bitterness one against the other—sour marriages, caustic tongues of unbroken wives, loveless husbands—much bitterness, all because there is no brokenness.

Brokenness releases life and brings about fruitfulness. Brokenness ultimately ministers energy to a fainting body through a process that initially may be very painful. That's the paradox; it is the pain that yields abundance.

God is interested in the breaking so that we might minister sweetness. He will break us, so that we can minister life more abundantly. God is in the breaking process so that we might be productive. We are broken so that we can offer energy, life, strength, and power. We are broken to be useful.

Jesus never sent forth any bread that He did not receive. He commissioned no bread that He did not break. The outcome of the open path ahead of each person is a function of what that person lets Him do with them today in His transforming laboratory we have chosen to call The Potter's House.

In Second Timothy 2:20, the Bible tells us that "in a great house" there are vessels of different types. In Jeremiah 18:6, the Great Potter Himself states that we all are like clay in His hands. He will do with us as He pleases, depending on the design He has in mind for each of us when He goes to work on us. In other words, even though we might all be vessels in His great house, we will not all be processed in the same way. Some will learn by simple observation. To these He might say, *"Follow Me."* Others carry a reproachful concealment that has long become a delicate part of their nature—a delicate part that has to be cut off. These will meet the slashing knife at Gilgal's slab. Others still must be broken and smashed before the beauty of His purpose may appear in their lives. These will go the way of the breaking process. Whatever way He may choose, His aim is the same—to make each of us into a glory for His display, better than when we came to Him. I pray that He will *find* you in order to *make* you.

SECTION THREE

CAUTION BEYOND THE POTTER'S HOUSE

Introduction

A book is remembered more often for how it ends than how it starts. We are a book that God is still writing. (See 2 Corinthians 3:1-3.) Often, the tricky devil, when he can no more stand the zeal of our early days, takes a break from those hot preliminary chapters of our lives. He then waits to put his foul pen to the closing details, so that, like Saul the first king of Israel, our story will end with an anticlimactic lamentation, "How art the mighty fallen...as though he had not been anointed with oil!" (2 Sam. 1:19-21). May God forbid it.

This is a call to caution, as the last chapter of our lives gets written beyond the Potter's House where the Master was at work on us. My prayer for all is that beyond the glamorous religious commitments of our amiable beginnings we would be careful not to let the devil write *the last chapter*.

The previous section of this book presented a panorama of different characters who passed through diverse processes in the preparation house of the Great Potter on their way to their divine purpose. Some by *following* through, others by *circumcision*, and others still by the *breaking* process were successfully made into the object of God's dream for them, despite the preliminary challenges that sought to frustrate that divine purpose. In this section, we will meet some who guarded their treasure beyond the Potter's House and others who, caught up in the mundane nature of everyday life, dropped their guard and missed the day of their destiny, passing on into history as if God had not had a mission for their lives.

Judas is remembered, not for the splendor of his call nor the devils he cast out in the company of the other disciples, but for how regrettably his life ended. For that reason, mothers and fathers of newborns shy away from the name Judas, preferring instead Judah or Jude, though these names all mean the same thing—praise. On the other hand, Rahab is celebrated not for her ignoble beginnings in the brothels of Jericho but for her glorious finish as the noble great-grandmother of kings. The same pattern holds for Saul, who became Paul. There are still many who proudly bear his name. No matter how well a race begins, no one celebrates unless it ends well.

What is the purpose of a great painting if it were concealed among the junk in an abandoned outhouse? Imagine all the time and talent invested in a masterpiece that is never exhibited in any way?

Once upon a time, God said to the prophet Elijah, "hide thyself" (1 Kings 17:3). Sometime later, the same God came to him and said, "Go, shew thyself" (1 Kings 18:1). There is a time to hide (or be hidden), but there also comes the time to step out and be seen. He calls us in to prepare us, in order to send us out to show forth His glory.

There comes a time to get away from men and the affairs of this life and be hidden in God's fashioning workshop. Afterward there will be a time that He will announce us to men. After His thirty silent years of waiting, just beyond His encounter with John the Baptist, the Voice from Heaven introduced Jesus with these words, "This is my beloved Son, in whom I am well pleased" (Matt. 3:17). Often, however, that announcement is the cue for the devil to test us, feverishly intervening with a Heaven-endorsed wilderness. The devil would love to win over us by having us close the story of our lives disgracefully. That is the flip side of what happens when we win over the devil and are gloriously publicized by God, beyond the times of hidden re-creative communing with the Divine.

"He *ordained* [called] twelve, that they should *be with Him* [to be made], and that He might *send them* forth to preach [to display them]" (Mark 3:14). He calls us, to take us in and make us as we follow Him, so that He might show us forth afterward to an expectant world.

As we learned in the previous section, even when God has enlisted us to make us, we still have our part to take care of. We must cautiously follow through the making process. Yet, the completion of our making does not place us into an untouchable display cupboard. We are only then confronted with a journey along whose routes we should display the splendor into which He has fashioned us. That is the caution that underscores "The Day You Must Not Miss." That is the allegory of Paul's missionary journey, which is the subject of "The Last Chapter."

CHAPTER 6

The Day You Must Not Miss

A Day of Destiny

There is a day in each person's life that will not come twice. To miss that day is to miss destiny. Unfortunately, that day doesn't ring a bell to announce its entry, and it doesn't give you time to prepare yourself. Still, it is the day you must not miss.

Some time ago, I met a troubled young man, who seemed to be having problems in his spiritual life. He told me this sad story. He was a medical student in the university, and the day came to take the compulsory major course in his qualifying medical exams. All his student years on that campus had been in preparation for that one day. He dreamed that someday he would become a medical doctor and would step out of the poverty into which he had been born. In pursuit of that dream, he had endured sleepless nights, completed all his assignments, read all his books. He'd even gone hungry at times, all for that one day. He had been awake the night before the exam, reading and studying. So, by morning, he had had little sleep.

About an hour before the time of the exam, he decided to take a short rest so he would be refreshed. When he woke up, he realized that he had slept much longer than he expected. He hurried down to the exam hall, but it was empty. To his shame and dismay, it was all over, irredeemably over. He had been preparing all night for an exam he never took.

Although he had a chance to repeat the exam the following year, he could not do it with the same motivation and enthusiasm. This time, he failed the course by just one point and could not graduate.

Oh, how he lamented that he would not be the doctor he had always dreamed of becoming because of one small mistake on one day of his life. He still remembers the day—the date, the year, the time—but he can never reverse his error. That day passed him by, leaving an indelible scar on his anguished destiny. It was one day in which he should have avoided his bed and stayed keenly aware of the time.

Every day does not pardon every sin that other days may have overlooked.

THE DAY OF JERUSALEM

In the Book of Luke, we find Jesus' sad lamentation over the city of Jerusalem. It is one of the only two occasions in the entire Bible where Jesus is said to have wept (the other being at the grave of Lazarus).

> *When He was come near, He beheld the city, and wept over it, saying, If thou hadst known, even thou, at least in this thy day, the things which belong unto thy peace! but now they are hid from thine eyes. For the days shall come upon thee, that thine enemies shall cast a trench about thee, and compass thee round, and keep thee in on every side, And shall lay thee even with the ground, and thy children within thee; and they shall not leave in thee one stone upon another; because thou knewest not the time of thy visitation (Luke 19:41-44).*

In verse 42, Jesus laments that there was something the city or the people of Jerusalem ought to have known. It was something which, even if they had failed to perceive it in previous centuries, they had no more excuse for failing to see. Yet it was not so much their persistent and tragic ignorance that He mourned; it was their inability to read the Clock of Heaven or hear the Heavenly Whistle announce the expiration of their season. He mourned for a people who, like a recalcitrant drunkard, were callously staggering past their day of grace.

One may imagine the feelings of Jesus, perhaps like the crushing weight of sad finality that stabs a desperate, losing champion soccer team after the referee's whistle seals their fate with its final blast at the end of regular time. The super striker not fielded until then could just as well have stayed in his bed. A hundred goals scored after that whistle are as useless as painted apples to a hungry man.

In the natural, for example, there are days designated in the calendar as World Leprosy Day, Mothers' Day, Thanksgiving Day, Children's Day, UNESCO Day for Refugees. On the calendar, these days come only once in a year. If you were to miss one of these days, you would have to wait a whole year for that day to come back around. In the calendar of eternity, however, that particular day might never come around again once missed. Or it might come around again but without the opportunities it once offered. That loss of opportunity seems to have been what drew the tears of Jesus.

As Jesus passed through Jerusalem that day, He noted that it was Jerusalem's day in the calendar of eternity. He described it as "this *thy* day." As a consequence of missing that day, Jesus said certain disasters would befall the city and people of that city. In verse 43, He said that because of missing that one day, other days would come, days in which their enemies would surround them, bring down their walls, crush them with their children, and tear down their monuments of pride one stone at a time. All this would happen because "thou knewest not the *time* of thy visitation" (Luke 19:43). In other words, this day is never missed without grave and enduring consequences.

It seems to me from this passage that everyone has a date in destiny with their name attached to it, a day of which it may be said, "this *thy* day."

There is a day in the calendar of eternity that has your name attached to it. There is a day in the calendar of eternity that has the name of your family attached to it. There is a day in the calendar of eternity that has the name of your city attached to it. There is a day in the calendar of eternity that has the name of your nation attached to it—a day which, if missed, might provoke eternal disaster and spell divine lamentations.

THE DAY OF JESUS

Hebrews 1:5 and 5:5 appear to speak of a day in the calendar of God that we may describe as the Day of Jesus. "Thou art My Son, *this day* have I begotten Thee? I will be to Him a Father, and He shall be to Me a Son" (Heb. 1:5). "So also Christ did not glorify Himself to become High Priest, but it was He who said to Him, 'You are My Son, *today* I have begotten You'" (Heb. 5:5, NKJV).

There are infinite days in the calendar of God, but there was one day in the destiny of Jesus that was referred to as "this day." That was the day God had marked from eternity to perform "the ceremony of begetting" for His only begotten Son.

I imagine that the Heavenly Father sent out invitation cards long in advance for that ceremony, and when the day finally came and the royal hall in Heaven had been decorated with flowers and chandeliers of pure crystal, the celestial guests were seated resplendently. I can see the seraphic caterers with their aprons poised in a corner of the hall. I can smell the aroma from their delicacies filling the palace, provoking anticipation among the impatient guests. I imagine also that the immaculate angelic ushers were at their posts by the golden gates and the marble pillars, everyone enjoying the choir of seraphim softly singing some of the celestial tunes they had been rehearsing for that very day (same as they sang in the sky of Bethlehem while shepherds watched their flocks on the night when Jesus was born on earth).

The atmosphere is electric with palpable expectations. But just then, there is an announcement over the loudspeakers, that like Queen Vashti of Persia, the Son has refused to show up because He thinks He ought Himself to have been the Father, not the Son.

Now close your eyes and imagine Scene II, the heavenly Master of Ceremonies has just asked the Son to step out and take His place by the Father. Thunderous applause is followed by blaring trumpets and stirring tones of the harp. All heads are turned in the direction of the expected celebrant. The ovation continues for a minute, five minutes, seven minutes, ten minutes, and then begins to die down as the crowd realizes no one is coming. An obviously embarrassed angel Michael confers frantically with the Father and goes back to the emcee. There is another announcement, "The Father expresses His regrets to the heavenly dignitaries. The ceremony is being postponed abruptly and indefinitely. The celebrant is nowhere to be found. Some speculate that He has gone to play golf on this important day."

We can never imagine the universal damage if that day had come and gone in vain, because the Son had failed to recognize the day of His visitation.

Where will you be when your day comes? I pray you won't be missing. Your day of destiny will be more important to you than an eternity of other days. One day may seem like another since the sun rises and sets on each. Today may be your day of destiny, your day of divine investiture, the day about which you can say, "this my day."

THE DAY OF SALVATION

*Wherefore (as the Holy Ghost saith, **To day** if ye will hear His voice, Harden not your hearts, as in the provocation, in the day of temptation in the wilderness:)... But exhort one another daily, while it is called **To day** lest any of you be hardened through the deceitfulness of sin.... While it is said, **To day** if ye will hear His voice, harden not your hearts, as in the provocation* (Hebrews 3:7-8,13,15).

Again, He limiteth [or designates] *a certain day, saying in David* [in the Psalms], ***To day**, after so long a time; as it is said, **To day** if ye will hear His voice, harden not your hearts"* (Hebrews 4:7).

These Bible passages appear to be saying, "You may harden your heart for fifteen or even fifty years and get away with it, but there comes for every person a 'today,' a limited or designated day, when that same apparently harmless rejection of God's salvation spells eternal disaster. This is a day beyond which the free salvation does not come so freely anymore." (See Hebrews 4:7.) Hebrews 3:13 appears to add that after that "day," there comes a *hardening* of the heart, through the satanic instrumentality of the deceitfulness of sin, a hardness of heart by which the rainbow of grace loses its appeal and seems rather like a log of repugnant lies.

Several years ago in my city, there used to be a fine Christian lady who got distracted by the pleasures of this life and walked out on God. Her later days without God were lived on the fast lanes of the Wide Road. With time, the liberties of the backslidden life got her into a relationship, and she became pregnant. Unfortunately, when the baby was due, there were complications, so she had to have a caesarean section. Sadly, because of the bleaching creams to which she had subjected her skin in her vanity to be fairer in complexion than she was (according to the popular trend in those days), her wounds would not heal properly, and a deadly infection set in.

Two weeks later, as she lay on the immaculate clinical bed in the General Hospital, death came. She began to scream, "Fire! Fire! Fire!" Only she could feel the heat and see the flames for which she agonized loud and long. Her aged mother who had been by her side in the hospital began to plead with her, "Pray, please, pray." But it seemed she could no longer pray. Her heart had hardened. The day of grace had passed. The God she used to love so much and with whom she used to talk so sweetly had gone so far away that her screams could not be heard. For several minutes she kept crying the same cry of agony, "Fire! Fire! Fire!" Gradually her voice began to die down like a call fading away in the distance. It seemed like the devil had caught her soul and was racing away with it, down the distant flaming corridors of eternity. Minutes later, her cries had fallen down to hardly perceptible whispers, "Fire! Fire! Fire!" With that woeful cry unfinished on her tiring lips, her soul slipped away into the everlasting flames of hell.

Alas, the day she took that turn away from the narrow path of the Lord, she made a terrible mistake! If she had known where that road would lead, she might not have let that day prey upon her precious soul.

I read a sad true story a few days ago. It happened in Mile Two, Lagos, Nigeria. As it is common, a young Christian man was preaching in one of those often-crowded sixty-seat intracity commuter buses popularly called *molue*. The bus had just stopped to pick up passengers and had hardly resumed its journey when a young man who had boarded with his girlfriend announced he intended to disembark at the next stop for the preacher's words were making him uncomfortable. The girlfriend protested, but the young man overruled her. As they were getting off at the next stop, the girl said to the preacher, "I enjoyed your preaching while my short trip lasted. I wish I could hear more." They got down and the bus took off. A few meters from there, the driver pulled into a petrol station. They were still waiting to refuel when that same young man who had alighted from the bus some minutes earlier ran breathlessly to them to narrate his story and confess his guilt. In the hurry to go across the busy expressway with the many speeding cars characteristic of Lagos roads, they had not watched carefully enough for oncoming vehicles. A speeding car hit them and the girl died on the spot.

She missed her last chance on her last day. She was never to know that, according to the calendar of eternity, that day was *her day*, her designated day. She may have rejected or postponed the Gospel many other days before, but that was one day not to have done the same thing. God saw the end had come for her and sent her a preacher, but.... Now for eternity, she will curse her soul and that young man who rushed her away. She might never find him in hell to vent her anger on him, because it was evident from the horror in his voice that he had begun to strongly consider the option of salvation, now that it was too late for her.

May it never be your lot to get a free ticket to hell, while the one who got you that ticket has changed flights on their way to heaven.

A pastor was going to travel but felt that the Lord was telling him not to drive in his car, so he took a taxi. Sitting with him at the back of the car were two girls who were engrossed in their conversation about fornication. The pastor used the opportunity to preach to them, but they responded that he had already "enjoyed" his life, and should let them become as old as he was before considering his message. While he still spoke to them and tried to convince them, there was an accident in which only two passengers died. Guess who? Those two girls. What would the conversation have been like if they had known it was their last day? "Again, he limiteth [or designates] a certain day, saying, 'To day if ye will hear His voice, harden not your hearts'" (Heb. 4:7).

They heard His voice. They hardened their hearts; but that day it was not without severe, irredeemable, and eternal consequences. Salvation is free, but there comes a time when even that free gift may not be so freely had anymore. The prophet warns in Isaiah 55:6, "Seek ye the Lord while He may be found, call ye upon Him while He is near." This would seem to say that there comes a time when God, who is now so close, will be so far away that the loudest loudspeakers would not be able to get His attention. It will be a time when the God who is now so present would have disappeared so abruptly that He can no more be found even with the aid of the best telescopes or microscopes.

There is a day of salvation with your name attached to it. This day, if missed, could have eternally grievous consequences. And that day may be now.

Tomorrow will always come, as long as Jesus tarries, but tomorrow does not come for everyone. For many, the hoped-for tomorrow turned out to be a bounced check, because there were no more future days in their "time account." Our days are numbered. They wasted theirs. David was not playing with words when he prayed, "So teach us to number our days, that we may apply our hearts unto wisdom" (Ps. 90:12).

THE DAY OF ABRAHAM

*It came to pass after these things that God **tested** Abraham, and said to him, "Abraham!" And he said, "Here I am." Then He said, "Take now your son, your only son Isaac, whom you love, and go to the land of Moriah, and offer him there as a burnt offering on one of the mountains of which I shall tell you" (Genesis 22:1-2 NKJV).*

The day came for God to promote Abraham, but not before He had "tested" him. No one goes to a higher class until all exams have been passed in the lower class. Strangely, God did not give Abraham any notice about this great exam, the result of which would qualify him to be described as the "father of all them that believe" (Romans 4:11). Examiners who prepare regular exams would issue a date and time, but for this exam there was none.

To say, "Take now your son...as a burnt offering" was hard enough, but to add, "your son, your only son," made it even more difficult. Then to go further still and add, "Isaac, whom you love," emphasized the humanly impossible nature of this deed. Three days would pass from the time Abraham received the instruction in his tent and his arrival on Mount Moriah with Isaac. This would have been quite enough time for most people to shake off the strange nightmare and change their minds. But Abraham did not change his mind. When the day came, he resolutely strapped his son to the altar of sacrificial obedience to Jehovah.

If I were that young man Isaac, I wonder if I would have let the old man go so far with me. After all, it was he who claimed that he had heard the voice of God; a God who had not consulted me to see if I also wanted to give away my life so early in the morning of my hopes. It is said that the pride of young men is their strength. I would have shown all of that strength that day in an Olympic race that I could not have afforded to lose.

Isaac was strapped helplessly to the altar. Frightened, the boy must have shut his eyes, so that he would not see the fatal blow as the knife rushed down on his tender throat. Abraham may also have shut his eyes or simply turned his face away, unable to look into the pleading eyes of his only son. Then the hand went up, trembling but determined. The razor edges of the knife glistened in the light of the morning sun in the eastern sky. In a moment the hand would begin its deadly descent, and Abraham knew he would hear the last sounds from his only son, the guttural groans of death and farewell. Abraham tightened his hold on the upraised knife, took a deep breath—and then a voice called out from Heaven, "Do not lay your hand on the lad, or do anything to him; for now I know that you fear God, since you have not withheld your son, your only son, from Me" (Gen. 22:12 NKJV).

What did God mean by "for *now* I know"? Doesn't God always know everything? Did He mean that all the days before "now" had been of little consequence to Him and the destiny of the man in question? Would the coming days after now be of less consequence? Does there come a "now day" in each of our lives when God says of us and of our commitment or betrayals, "for now I know"?

God knows everything, but it seems to me that in our work and walk with Him, we each come to a point where through our triumph or failure, God has to declare to all of creation, "for now I know." This is a declaration by which our vanities become not only apparent to men and devils and angels, but our fate is eternally sealed. Or it is a triumphant declaration by which He issues us our sealed Certificate of Blessings, which opens for us the door into the things that for long had been mere promises. Thereafter, if satanic principalities and powers should query why God would call us fathers (or sons) of faith, or if anyone should question why He should thus bless us beyond measure (or not bless us at all), the Righteous Judge would simply show them the certificate of our performance on *that* day, asserting why we have been placed where we are in destiny.

For Abraham, the day of his son's sacrifice (for God did credit him with the sacrifice even though it was averted) marked the turning point in his destiny. Generations later, we continue to look back at that one day that he *did not miss*. Who knows, Abraham's story may have ended in that chapter if he had missed that day.

Many other days may still have come after that, but not with the same opportunity in the same way.

Abraham had done many things for God before that day in Genesis 22. He had obeyed God enough already to be where he was then, but all of that, it seemed, had been merely probationary sacrifice, probationary obedience. The one day was coming when it would be proved whether or not he should be offered his Certificate of Blessings and conferred with the prestigious award of "father of all them that believe." That day was the day he was asked to offer up his son Isaac. That day was the key to his destiny.

God does not always tell us when He is about to test us. Sometimes, those things that our commitment to God threatens to take from us are merely the key to the greater things it is bringing to us.

THE DAY OF ESAU

This "day" of which we speak often comes as a day of great paradoxes, a day of great trials as well as a day of great opportunities. This depends on which side of the day a person places himself or herself by their response. The day came for it to be decided in the heavens if Esau, the first son of Isaac, was qualified to be invested with the blessings of the firstborn. The testing came in the form of a strange hunger at the end of a tiring day. When he got home, his sly brother was in the kitchen preparing food designed to tempt even a reluctant appetite. Perhaps as he often did, Esau staggered over to his brother and asked to be served. But on this day, his brother informed him that the food was for sale in the currency of the birthright of a first son. The hungry Esau may have dismissed the proposition thinking the birthright was not his to lose. After all, he was born first and there was no changing that. He would always be the elder no matter what he might promise his brother. Such things could not be undone. So he sealed the deal with an oath and sat down to eat, never really considering what he had given up.

The years rolled by as if nothing had happened, but the day of reckoning eventually came when the blessings of the first son were to be pronounced. That's when the meal-deal of long ago loomed large and the blessing was given to Jacob. Esau had lost out all because of one hungry day.

That may not have been the first time Esau had eaten a meal like that, but the meal on that day was one he should not have eaten. He could not on that day do the things that he had done on other days without adverse consequences. After that day, other days came, but those many days did not come with the opportunity he had forever lost. (See Genesis 25:29–26:1; 27:30-45.)

> *Lest there be any fornicator, or profane person, as Esau, who for one morsel of meat sold his birthright. For ye know how that afterward, when he would have inherited the blessing, he was rejected: for he found no place of repentance, though he sought it carefully with tears* (Hebrews 12:16-17).

After he lost the blessing, Esau probably became much more careful, especially concerning that devilish delicacy called "Jacob's hamburger," but he was careful too late. The Bible says that he sought *"carefully with tears"* the day he had lost, but they were futile tears. If only he had been careful when his day came! Had he not blundered on that day, we might now be speaking of "the God of Abraham, the God of Isaac, and the God of Esau."

When Esau traded his eternal blessings for a temporary meal, he not only lost the blessing for his own life but also for his children and grandchildren down through the generations. His thoughtless decision impacted their lives as well, leaving them stranded and bereft of their eternal inheritance. Could just one forgotten meal on one day become such an eternal memorial of denial in the life of a man?

Sometimes we fail to value what we have until we have it no more. A deferred caution might be a disaster. Many late tears may never wash away the stains of a deliberate sin. Forgiveness is God's promise to the one who would repent, but sometimes, even a profound confession comes too late to repair the ruins of a deliberate barter of the soul.

THE DAY OF JOSEPH

It was a day of great temptation as well as a day of great blessing. It was a day of distractions as well as a day of focus. It was the day when Joseph sealed his destiny whether to die as the chief servant in Potiphar's house or become the Prime Minister of Egypt.

Joseph had endured the betrayal of his brothers and slavery in a strange land. He had avoided the seductions of youth, all in anticipation of a future day when, according to his dream, men would bow down to him. But that day was not going to come easily. First would come a day of great temptation. His master's wife, having shown unusual interest in him, lavished him with compliments and became desperately passionate. She wanted him in her bed.

How many young men would not jump at such a privilege with all the promises of promotion added to the package? What was there to lose if he conceded? Indeed, there seemed to be so much to gain—less labor (as the consort of the Madam), better meals (almost like the master of the house), and more prestige among his fellow slaves. It might even be the fulfillment of his dreams that royalty—like the stars, the moon and the sun—would bow to him. But another voice said quickly to him, "No, this is your one chance to prove your integrity, even if you have to suffer for it."

He mustered the courage at last to confront the sin that had personified itself before him in the form of the mistress of the house, and he said somewhat bluntly to her, "There is none greater in this house than I; neither hath he kept back any thing from me but thee, because thou art his wife: how then can I do this great wickedness, and sin against God?" (Gen. 39:9).

How dare Joseph bring God into this matter? Was he defending the name of God so far away in this strange land? Was he speaking of the same God who had not protected him from the malice of his brothers? How could he describe Madam's offer not merely as "wickedness" but as *"great* wickedness?" From what different perspective did he look at the world?

That was his day, but it came in the form of a great trial. He had to choose between imprisonment and promotion. Mrs. Potiphar was the T-junction in his journey. He could have gone softly left into a temporary pleasure island or stubbornly right through the tunnel of affliction and into God's purpose for his life. She was the bend in his road. He would either go to his palace of destiny through the inevitable prison of preparation or to her pampered kitchen of quick but temporary pleasure as an elevated slave. He chose the more difficult but righteous option. Years later, the king looked for him in the prison where his enemies had hoped to leave him abandoned and forgotten.

I pray that kings will look for you when your day comes and God will favor you in spite of the fact that you have been abandoned and forgotten by those who hope to ruin you.

Had Joseph succumbed to Mrs. Potiphar's seductions, he could have been munching himself fat in her "kitchen of perpetual limitation," while destiny searched in vain for him in the "prison of temporary but productive pain." Destiny would now usher him into the palace of reward as Egypt's prime minister. Who knows how many prime ministers and kings have ended up in somebody's kitchen or backyard, their journey to the throne truncated once upon a terrible day by forbidden fruit from which they should have fled!

Joseph excelled where, years before, Reuben his eldest brother had failed, forfeiting the blessing of the first son and earning instead a curse when the day came to invest him with the glory. Apparently, when Reuben lost the day, it passed over, with all its benefits, to Joseph. His dying father's voice pronounced the verdict that was to haunt Reuben for the rest of his life. He had missed the day, that one important day that determined his destiny.

> Reuben, thou art my firstborn, my might, and the beginning of my strength, the excellency of dignity, and the excellency of power: Unstable as water, thou shalt not excel; because thou wentest up to thy father's bed; then defiledst thou it: he went up to my couch (Genesis 49:3-4).

Imagine how you would feel if those were your father's last words. Can you picture the scene? Reuben and his brothers are standing around their father Isaac's death bed. Then Jacob addresses Reuben by name and brings up an incident that had happened many years before. Reuben had blundered by sleeping with one of his father's wives. Jacob went on to swear before everyone that Reuben would not amount to anything because of the shame he had brought to their home. Then he passed over Reuben completely and gave the blessing of the firstborn to his younger brother Joseph. Reuben must have thought he was trapped in a bad dream.

A few minutes of illicit pleasure with his father's wife stole Reuben's eternal deposit of legitimate blessings. What a terrible bargain! His children, lining up behind him into eternity, watched in disappointment as the favor that should have been passed to them went elsewhere because of that one day when Reuben failed!

The pleasure you now pursue heedlessly may tomorrow take from you much more than it ever promised.

THE DAY OF ISAIAH

I was thinking about the landmark experience of the Prophet Isaiah, as recorded in the sixth chapter of his book, when God showed up in the awesome glory that transformed his life to prepare him for the next level. Suppose the prophet had excused himself when God came calling? What if he had told God to come back some other time, some other day? What would have been that prophet's story then? If Isaiah had missed that day, he could have missed the gateway into his purpose in life.

In the year that King Uzziah died, I saw the Lord seated on a throne, high and exalted, and the train of His robe filled the temple. Above Him were seraphs, each with six wings: With two wings they covered their faces, with two they covered their feet, and with two they were flying. And they were calling to one another: "Holy, holy, holy is the Lord Almighty; the whole earth is full of His glory." At the sound of their voices the doorposts and thresholds shook and the temple was filled with smoke. "Woe to me!" I cried. "I am ruined! For I am a man of unclean lips, and I live among a people of unclean lips, and my eyes have seen the King, the Lord Almighty." Then one of the seraphs flew to me with a live coal in his hand, which he had taken with tongs from the altar. With it he touched my mouth and said, "See, this has touched your lips; your guilt is taken away and your sin atoned for." Then I heard the voice of the Lord saying, "Whom shall I send? And who will go for Us?" And I said, "Here am I. Send me!" He said, "Go" (Isaiah 6:1-8 NIV).

How could any mortal duplicate this? Who could gather again all those angels to repeat that awesome millennial service? In what temple? And could anyone also summon God back, and make Him call again, "Whom shall I send?" so that Isaiah would have another chance to say, "Here am I, send me"? What mortal could call back again the shekinah of God, in whose brightness Isaiah had seen his own shame so clearly that he could cry, "Woe is me!" And yet that's what happened, giving Heaven the opportunity to process his lips so he could go on to the next level. It was more than a once-in-a-lifetime experience; it was a once-in-the-Bible experience. There is no record anywhere in the Bible of this happening again.

If Isaiah had missed that day, therefore, that would have been it for him. He still could have gone on being a prophet, but while men celebrated his "great ministry," only God would have known what a far cry he was from what he could have been if he had not missed his day.

A pastor friend told me that he had received a word from God instructing him to visit a particular city to pray that the yoke of barrenness would be broken and those women who had had delays in childbearing would have babies. In obedience, a meeting was called in that city, during which formerly barren women were called out and prayed for. Miraculously, all the women who were prayed for soon became pregnant and had babies. The same pastor has had invitations to return to that city and repeat that meeting, but he has not gone. Why? Because God has not sent him back there. Like Jerusalem, that meeting represented the day of that city's visitation, "This thy day…the time of thy visitation" (Luke 19:42,44).

Let us imagine that some woman had not attended that meeting because she wanted a more private setting or had been absent because she had some urgent business that same day. Suppose she were rich enough to hire a hall all by herself and fly the pastor back (and the pastor himself were foolish enough to be lured by her hire), could she also have hired God back or rewound the clock?

A certain woman in another city met the same man of God with her problem of childlessness, but he did not pray for her as he had the others. Instead he asked her to jump up three times and go home. She did, and in due season she had her first baby. Afterward, she returned to the same man of God because she wanted another baby. She was ready to jump some more; as many times as the man would ask. But he told her that it was not about jumping; it was about God's unction and timing. The anointing that moved him that day had gone with the day. The anointing was not something he carried about in his pocket and operated whenever he wanted, like a toy.

Suppose this lady had ignored the man's initial instructions to jump and was now returning on her own day to make up for what was missed. Oh how sadly she would have gone back home, regretting the chance she had sought all her barren years and lost at last on a day that would never return!

It reminds me of the story of the man they called "Blind Bartimaeus." He hoped God would one day roll away that reproachful name men had stamped him with. Days upon days (only God knows how many days), he had dreamed that the day would come when he would meet the great Prophet Jesus, of whom he had heard so many things; and he hoped that on that day his blind eyes would be opened.

Every day he listened to the crowds as they passed by, but they did not have the characteristic signature of the multitudes of Jesus. He waited. Then one day it happened. He heard the noise of a passing multitude. When he enquired, he was told that Jesus was passing by. He mustered all his strength and began to call out, "Jesus, thou Son of David, have mercy on me" (Mark 10:47). Then the crowd turned upon him and began to crush him with one giant voice, urging him to shut up his filthy mouth and stop disturbing the peace of decent and civil men. He must have thought within himself, "If I do not take advantage of this chance, I might not have another. Those people shouting at me may have other chances, because this may not be *their* day, but it could be *my* day, my only day." So he kept shouting, "Jesus, thou Son of David, have mercy on me!" (Mark 10:48 NIV).

That was his first chance, his last chance, and his only chance. Jesus was on His way out of that city on His way to die. He never passed that way again.

> *"Shut up!" some of the people yelled at him. But he only shouted the louder, again and again, "O Son of David, have mercy on me!" When Jesus heard him, He stopped there in the road and said, "Tell him to come here." So they called the blind man. "You lucky fellow," they said, "come on, He's calling you!" Bartimaeus yanked off his old coat and flung it aside, jumped up and came to Jesus* (Mark 10:48-50 TLB).

Jesus stopped to give that socially despicable blind man His divine attention, and the man received his sight. Had Bartimaeus given in to the pressure of the crowd, he could have missed his day. While others walked on to meet their own day in the future, he would have remained blind for life.

I pray that you will not allow anyone to stop you when your day comes.

THE DAY OF KING SAUL

The story of Saul, the first king of Israel, is a story that waves a banner of caution in the face of anyone whom God has called. It is the ironic and tragic story of a young man who begins with much promise in his life, but whose sad end is lamented, "How art the mighty fallen...as though he was not anointed with oil" (2 Sam. 1:19,21).

It all began when the Israelites decided they wanted a king. God granted their request and found someone for the throne. The man He found was the best there was in the land, "an impressive young man without equal among the Israelites" (1 Sam. 9:2 NIV). God had to tamper with the smooth running of Saul's father's business just to get Saul's attention and move him to the place of the anointing. Saul was anointed with great fanfare, as the first king of Israel, and the hopes of all were very high. (See 1 Samuel 9-10.)

Although Saul had been made king, it would appear that his *establishment* as king or entrance into the fullness of his office was not automatic. It was to follow what, in the jargon of contemporary politics and conceptions of fairness, would be described as "due process."

The people had been told in First Samuel 11 that they would "go to Gilgal, and *renew* the kingdom there" (1 Sam. 11:14). According to the Living Bible, the mission to Gilgal was to "*reconfirm* Saul as our king." The New International Version uses the word *reaffirm*. So, the people went to Gilgal for the great ceremony of reconfirming Saul as king. There, everyone awaited the prophet Samuel who was to conduct the ceremony. He had stipulated seven days for his arrival. Strangely, however, that day of "confirmation" for Saul, unlike the day of his coronation, did not come as a day of ceremony. It came as a day of confrontation with Israel's sworn enemies, the Philistines. "Saul remained at Gilgal, and all the troops with him were quaking with fear. He waited seven days, the time set by Samuel; but Samuel did not come to Gilgal, and Saul's men began to scatter" (1 Sam. 13:7-8 NIV).

Especially in public and civil service, a person is sometimes given a job on "probation," which means that the person would serve a stipulated trial period (maybe six months or two years), before they are "confirmed," that is, before they are absorbed or "initiated" into full membership of the organization with all benefits, and treated like regular staff members. It would appear that Saul was crowned on probation, after which the Gilgal ceremony of confirmation as "king forever" was to come.

Saul served his two-year probation but failed the qualifying exam that should have kept him permanently on the throne. In First Samuel 13:1-2, we read, "Saul reigned one year; and when he had reigned two years over Israel, Saul chose him three thousand men of Israel."

When did Saul choose his three thousand men? It was "when he had reigned two years." In other words, the events in chapter 13 took place after the second year of Saul's reign. At least we can date that chapter to after the second year of Saul's reign. What happened in that season? Saul chose three thousand soldiers, a war threatened to break out with the Philistines, the prophet Samuel asked the new king to wait seven days for him in Gilgal, and God terminated the tenure of Saul as king.

The king made some blunders while he waited, although he excused himself and blamed everyone else. The grave significance of the king's failure that day becomes apparent when the prophet arrives on the scene and announces to the self-excusing culprit:

> *Thou hast done foolishly: thou hast not kept the commandment of the Lord thy God, which he commanded thee: for now would the Lord have established thy kingdom upon Israel for ever. But now thy kingdom shall not continue: the Lord hath sought Him a man after His own heart, and the Lord hath commanded him to be captain over His people, because thou hast not kept that which the Lord commanded thee* (1 Samuel 13:13-14).

After the new king's two years of mandatory probation, God issued the prophet the stamp of approval to be put on the appointment letter of the king, but Saul had to pass one more endurance test. For that reason, perhaps, God delayed Samuel to see if the absence of the prophet could become a justification for error in the life of Saul. By the time the prophet arrived, the king had failed and the crowd that had assembled for the reaffirmation ceremony had begun to scatter. There at Gilgal, the prophet Samuel had the unpleasant task of announcing Heaven's grave verdict on the failed king.

There are many implications of the prophet's monumental statement. First, when the prophet said, "for *now* [or today] would the Lord have established thy kingdom upon Israel for ever," it seems to me that He was saying Saul's day had come in spite of all of Saul's previous achievements or failures. (See 1 Samuel 13:13.) Unfortunately, the man blamed his failure that day on everyone else, even the prophet of God, without knowing what was at stake. God could have answered Saul and said, "I was the One who de-layed Samuel, because I wanted to see how you would react under pressure. Do not blame him; blame yourself. You were the person under investigation. It was for your sake that I frustrated his efforts to arrive on time. *Now I know.*"

Second, as a consequence of Saul's failure that day, God found a replacement to the eternal throne of Israel. That replacement was David, the son of Jesse. The prophet announced to the expiring king, "But now thy kingdom shall not continue: the Lord hath sought him [another] man" (1 Sam. 13:14). So, that day, which had been scheduled as a day for confirming Saul as the perpetual king of Israel, became a day of divine replacement. For one, it became the end of the road; for the other, it became the beginning of a jour-ney. For one, it was the abortion of an eternal mandate; for the other, it was the conception of a new dream. Alas, the paradox of one great day!

In Acts 13:21 we read, "Then the people asked for a king, and He gave them Saul son of Kish, of the tribe of Benjamin, who ruled forty years" (NIV). According to First Samuel 13, as has been shown above, Saul was rejected in his second year. And yet he "ruled forty years." This can only mean that the man had gone on for another thirty-eight years running his own show, without the God with whom he had started. Is that possible? It would mean that, while the elder Saul had the title of "king," the younger David was actually the person whom Heaven recognized in that office. Was Saul merely marking time on the throne while God groomed David to step in when His time was right?

There are many today who, like Saul, parade titles that Heaven recognizes no more. Many of these people seek a name rather than the glory of God. It is not a matter of fancy titles; it is a matter of whom Heaven has approved.

Third, we read that if Saul had not blundered on that day, he could have been the king *over Israel forever*. If Saul remained a king *forever*, there would not have been a David. That may suggest that David, who became Saul's replacement, was not in God's original plan, although as the alternative, he turned out to be better than the original. From the prophet's revelation, it would appear that if Saul had not had an abortion of destiny that day, he could have been succeeded by his own son Jonathan, and Jonathan might then have been succeeded by his son Ishboshet, and so on and on in the same way we speak today of the throne of David. But all that was to pass away because of the failure of a man on a day that God simply described twice as "now." Alas, how swiftly the destiny of thousands of people yet unborn was wasted in one day by one man!

Years later, like Esau, Saul did everything in his royal power to try to reverse the verdict of Heaven. He plotted several times to kill David, his divine replacement. He sought to position his son Jonathan for the throne. But all his schemes were belated efforts. In frustration, he ended up cursing that same son when in anger he said, "Thou son of the perverse rebellious woman, do not I know that thou hast chosen the son of Jesse to thine own confusion, and unto the confusion of thy mother's nakedness?" (1 Sam. 20:30).

Eventually, the time came to write the epilogue on this king who had started so gloriously in his probationary years that it was wondered aloud, "Is Saul also among the prophets?" (1 Sam. 10:11). Unfortunately, we find a paradox in this last chapter. The man who at his beginning had prophesied among prophets was in his last days found in the sanctuary of a notable witch, partaking in a strange unholy communion of "unleavened bread" and a counterfeit lamb which had been slain. (See 1 Samuel 28:24-25.) We also read that this man who used to prophesy so remarkably with elder prophets had become such a reprobate that God would no more talk to him, "neither by dreams nor by Urim, nor by prophets" (1 Sam. 28:6). We discover also that this man who began his journey at the house of the prophet Samuel in a morning of hope had walked into a "night" at the house of a witch—a night that eventually brought about his death on the mountain of Gilboa.

Gilboa means "bubbling fountain." Ironically, that was where his bubbles died. The last song for Saul was nothing like the one we heard in the beginning when the people sang the proverb, "Is Saul also among the prophets?" The final song was a sad dirge, which lamented:

> *The beauty of Israel is slain upon thy high places: how are the mighty fallen! Tell it not in Gath, publish it not in the streets of Askelon; lest the daughters of the Philistines rejoice, lest the daughters of the uncircumcised triumph. Ye mountains of Gilboa, let there be no dew, neither let there be rain, upon you, nor fields of offerings: for there the shield of the mighty is vilely cast away, the shield of Saul, as though he had not been anointed with oil. From the blood of the slain, from the fat of the mighty, the bow of Jonathan turned not back, and the sword of Saul returned not empty. Saul and Jonathan were lovely and pleasant in their lives, and in their death they were not divided: they were swifter than eagles, they were stronger than lions. Ye daughters of Israel, weep over Saul, who clothed you in scarlet, with other delights, who put on ornaments of gold upon your apparel. How are the mighty fallen in the midst of the battle! O Jonathan, thou was slain in thine high places. I am distressed for thee, my brother Jonathan: very pleasant hast thou been unto Me: thy love to Me was wonderful, passing the love of women. How are the mighty fallen, and the weapons of war perished! (2 Samuel 1:19-27)*

How well one starts is not always a promise for how well one ends.

THE DAY OF SAMSON

In Nigeria, we have a pidgin proverb, which states, *"One day, one day, monkey go go market e no go return,"* which means almost the same as "Every day for the thief, *one day* for the owner."

Samson was a great man who took grace for granted. One day he went on a mission after an attractive girl in the enemy territory of Philistia. God sent a young lion to intercept him with a warning. He killed that little messenger and made a great proverb out of the cat, but did not catch on to the message (Judges 14). On that mission, Samson, in various forms, paid a huge bride price for a girl he never married. Next, along the same Philistine highway, in pursuit of another Philistine girl, this time a prostitute, God saved him from a close shave with death at the gates of Gaza. (See Judges 16:1-3.) But even that was not enough warning for Samson. Maybe he had said to himself, "If I did it so cleverly yesterday and got away with it, I guess I am wise enough to try it again." He did not know when his last day of grace came. That day found him in the valley of Sorek with his head on the lap of Delilah, the notorious seductress. He had thought that physical strength was everything, but he was to learn there were other powers stronger than brawn.

Drunk with lust and deaf to the pleading voice of the Holy One, he staggered out of Delilah's chamber one morning and announced proudly in the face of his enemies, "I will go out as at other times before, and shake myself" (Judg. 16:20). There is a lot of "I" and "me" and "myself" in that speech, and nothing of God. How much unlike the Shepherd's Psalm that sounds. "The Lord is My shepherd, He maketh…He leadeth…He restoreth" (see Ps. 23). And yet it does sound like the manifesto of lucifer who said, "I will ascend into heaven, I will exalt my throne above the stars of God: I will sit...I will ascend...I will be" (Isa. 14:13-14).

Samson, while he so relied on his past exploits, did not know that grace had expired. He did not know that physical strength was not everything. He did not know that a day had come at last unlike any of the other days in Timnath and Gaza. On those days, he had done the same things and gotten away without suffering the consequences. Today was his last day, and "the Lord was departed from him" (Judg. 16:20). He had not heard the referee's whistle nor noticed when he was issued his last yellow card. His descent that day down the Sorek valley into Delilah's oriental suite was going to be his last move in those careless games, but he never knew.

It is said that "he awoke out of his sleep" that day to attempt the challenge, but he woke up too late. He paid for it with his eyes, never more to sleep in the house of a sworn enemy, no matter how seemingly friendly. That day which he took for granted like all the other days turned out to be no more his day, but the day of the Philistines, his enemies. It was the day of their songs, when *they praised their god*" and sang against him, saying, "Our god hath delivered into our hands our enemy, and the destroyer of our country, which slew many of us" (Judg. 16:24). He lost the day, and his enemies took it from him and made the most of it.

Days, or probably, weeks later, when his hair began to grow again, he prayed for a rematch with those same enemies so that he could at least regain some of his lost honor. This time he would go into the bout without his eyes. This was his prayer, "O Lord God, remember me, I pray thee, and strengthen me, I pray thee, only this once, O God, that I may be at once avenged of the Philistines for my two eyes" (Judg. 16:28).

He died a hero, but he died a blinded hero. Imagine what a glorious end he could have had if he had not wasted his day.

THE DAY OF ESTHER

Sometimes God secures a *today* for His people because of a *tomorrow* He seeks to avert. That may describe the story of Esther, the young immigrant girl who became queen of the most powerful empire of her day.

Esther was taken into the royal house of Ahasuerus (Xerxes), king of Persia "in the tenth month [of] the seventh year" of his reign (see Esther 2:16). In the first month of "the twelfth year" of the same king's reign, Honorable Haman, Chief of Protocols in the palace, began to grow in prominence. This man was raised up by satan to exterminate the Jews. (See Esther 3:6.) In other words, more than five years before Haman began to show his mischievous head, our omniscient God had planted one of His own on the throne. Sadly, however, when the season came for which God had been planning, Esther was in danger of being distracted by the comfort and privileges of the "waiting room" of queenship in which destiny had concealed her. She and her congregation of ladies had been wining and dining while their city mourned the spell of death that Haman had cast over it. (See Esther 3:15.)

Things would have kept moving in the direction of a monumental tragedy had not God sent to her Mordecai, His servant, an elder at the gate. He explained why God had placed her in the palace of the king. Mordecai would not be intimidated by the barricades of protocol and royalty that privilege had surrounded her with. Mordecai sent the young queen a blunt message; warning her that her season had come. If she missed it, failing to understand the importance of what was happening, her father's house (irrespective of the royal immunity she thought she enjoyed at the moment) would suffer a terrible disaster, one she was in a position to prevent. Mordecai said to her:

> *Do not think that because you are in the king's house you alone of all the Jews will escape. For if you remain silent at this time,*

relief and deliverance for the Jews will arise from another place, but you and your father's family will perish. And who knows but that you have come to royal position for such a time as this? (Esther 4:13-14 NIV)

For some, what destiny has marked on their calendar is a day, but for others, it is a season. Both are all about time, fleeting time. For this queen, it was about a certain season of time. The elder at the gate was specific about the issue when, in his short speech, he hinted twice at the matter of "time."

Then Esther bade them return Mordecai this answer, Go, gather together all the Jews that are present in Shushan, and fast ye for me, and neither eat nor drink three days, night or day: I also and my maidens will fast likewise; and so will I go in unto the king, which is not according to the law: and if I perish, I perish (Esther 4:15-16).

Thank God, Esther awoke to her season with just a little prodding from Mordecai. There are many more women like Esther who need the prodding of the voice of the elders at the gate. May God today send them that voice and trouble them out of their sleep before the sun sets over them, bringing their day to a dismal close.

There was a season coming for Esther, one season for which God had been preparing her. For all the security she had enjoyed, the popularity she had known, the special convoys she rode in, the peace and comfort she had enjoyed, there was coming just one season when she was to perform the one responsibility for which God had invested all those privileges into her life. If she missed that season, all the investments of God would have been made in vain.

A friend lately remarked to me that a sprinter trains for several hours every day for several years, just to run for a few seconds on one day! How true! The man who spends just a few seconds a day preparing for the race will never get to the Olympics. Much practice, many months, even years, go into the successful race that is over in just a few seconds. It was said of Martin Luther King Jr. that he would prepare for eighteen hours to deliver a short speech of eighteen minutes. No wonder his words were so powerful and continue to be today.

Jesus trained for thirty years for a ministry that would last only three and a half years. It takes years of preparation to run well for a few seconds on Olympic day. Those who are winners on the day of the Olympic race were not made on that day. Likewise, the season of Esther's unveiling was a product of previous seasons of preparation.

Imagine this. A national committee invests years in the preparation of an athlete to compete in the Olympic Games. On the day of the race, everyone is glued to their TV screens waiting anxiously for their athlete to bring home the gold medal. The names of the runners and the nations they represent are blasted from the loudspeakers as everyone applauds loudly for their favorite. Then they call the name of the contestant who should be wearing your national colors, "Esther Xerxes from the United Republic of...." Everyone begins to cheer, but soon, there is silence because Esther does not appear. The race goes on in spite of her vacant lane. In the end, some less endowed runner takes home the gold. A day later, the headlines carry the shameful news that your golden Esther had been having a date with a new boyfriend in the night club next door to the Olympic stadium. If you were the president of the Olympic committee of her country or her fellow countryman, what would you say to this Esther when the flight brings her home after the Games?

The Esther of the Bible was not unprepared when her season came. She only needed someone to stir her up. Sometimes even mighty men need other men to wake them up, hence the call by the prophet Joel to "wake up the mighty men" (Joel 3:9). Esther arose and saved her people. And because she identified her day and seized it with both hands when it came, another day of memorial was born in her honor, the Day of Esther, which is the annual Feast of Purim. On this day every year, her people, the Jews, remember her intervention.

Will there be any day on the calendar of your village or your city or your street that will celebrate you because you rose up to meet your day when it came? For what will you be remembered when your days on earth have rolled to a close?

THE SEASONS OF THE AMALEKITES

For some, it is a day not to miss; for others, it is a season. In a sense, days never return, once they have passed. Consider, for example, the massacre that took place in Liberia on Sunday, September 9, 1990, resulting from the tri-factional national crises in which President Samuel Doe was killed the following day; or the tragedy that occurred on September 11, 2001, when the twin towers of the World Trade Center were destroyed in New York City. Those two days will never come around again with the same opportunity to do things differently. On the other hand, seasons, like summer and winter, the dry and rainy seasons, the Christmas season, will return each year. They represent a larger, more general chunk of days. Yet even seasons, with their particular collective ceremonial activities do pass away, though not as specifically as days do.

A day or a date might be significant as someone's birthday, but a season like winter or Christmas is unique not just to an individual but to communities of people. In other words, a day might be more or less private, but seasons are more communal, in terms of the collection of people that they affect.

In the days of Moses and Joshua, God swore to "utterly put out the remembrance of Amalek from under heaven" (Exod. 17:14). A few verses later, Moses explained *how* God would do *what* He had said He would do: through seasonal wars, "from generation to generation" (see verse 16). God declared His intent, Moses explained the process. That process began with the generation of Amalekites in the days of Moses and Joshua.

Sometime later, in the days of the Simeonites, and later still in the days of David, the season of the Amalekites came round again. But the most significant season of the Amalekites was in the days of Saul, the first king of Israel. In that season, God, after introducing Himself by His military title of "the Lord of hosts," announced, "I remember that which Amalek did…" (as if a day of remembrance had come, even though God does not forget). Then God proceeded to order King Saul to "utterly destroy all" (1 Sam. 15:2-3). That was supposed to be the last generation of Amalekites. But in that season, Saul failed to deal the last blow, and the people of God were forced to wait another 600 years before that season would come around again. Unfortunately, when it came, it came like a double-edged sword. Haman, who devised the plot against the Jews that was squelched by Queen Esther, was a descendant of the Amalekite king, Agag.

In King Saul's botched mission against the Amalekites of his generation or season, he spared the very king of the people whom he had been told to exterminate. We find out later that not only the king but other notable people as well were spared in direct disobedience to God's instruction. Meanwhile, Saul had given himself an elaborate passing grade for his activities that day—that is until the prophet showed up with God's opinion of Saul's actions.

The prophet Samuel had to take upon himself the task of completing Saul's unfinished mission. As Samuel the prophet executed on Agag the judgment from God that Saul had unilaterally waived, he proclaimed prophetically to Agag, "As thy sword hath made women childless, so shall thy mother be childless among women" (1 Sam. 15:33). The prophet's statement suggests that the queen mother (Agag's mother) had also been spared even though she had not been subjected to the long, rigorous trek back to Israel. Years later, David had to war with some of the remnant Amalekites. (See 1 Samuel 30.)

If Saul had obeyed the Lord and wiped them out, they would not have been there to trouble David in later years. Yet David was not the only one those remnant seeds troubled. They showed up again to threaten the whole nation of Jews during the reign of Queen Esther some 600 years after Saul.

Haman the Agagite, in the days of Esther, was the last of the giants surviving from the disobedience of Saul six centuries before. We find in Numbers 24:7 and First Samuel 15 that Agag was the title of the kings of Amalek, just as Pharaoh was the title of the kings of Egypt. When, therefore, the Bible describes the wicked Haman as an "Agagite," this signified that he was not an ordinary Amalekite, but a surviving seed from the royal line. (See Esther 8:3.) He was an Agagite Amalekite, who having found himself a place in the Persian palace, plotted to exterminate the remnant seeds of those who would not exterminate his fathers when they had their day in the time of King Saul.

This is what happens when we miss our season. The season may come around again, but not with the same opportunities. In fact, because we did not deal with things properly in our season, they may pose an even greater threat the next time.

In the previous season, God had raised a man, a king from the tribe of Benjamin, to give the final blow to the Amalekites. (See 1 Samuel 9:1-2.) That man was King Saul. He failed. This time, God raised up a young woman, a queen from the same tribe of Benjamin, to complete the task that the earlier Benjamite man had left undone. (See Esther 2:5.) That woman was Esther the Queen, who restored songs back to the sighing lips of her people as they mourned the harvest of the disobedience that Saul had sown hundreds of years before when he had failed to read the signs of the time.

What does it mean to understand the times?

The Bible speaks in First Chronicles 12:32 of "the men of Issachar, who understood the times and knew what Israel should do" (NIV). To "know the times" is to know what is to be done.

What point is there in announcing the time if we do not know what we are to do at that time? The clock becomes merely a decoration to the one who turns over and over in bed, reading the face of that time piece hour after hour from under a blanket bunker, but doing nothing with the information. To understand the times is to know what *should* be done and to be ready to do it.

Esther, with the help of Mordecai, the elder at the gate, understood her season, and she grabbed it. Saul, in spite of the prophet Samuel, could not read the signs of the time and planted a seed that would threaten his people centuries later.

"Open thou mine eyes, [O Lord]" (Ps. 119:18).

CHRONOS AND KAIROS

The Greeks actually had two separate words for time. One was *chronos*; that is, time as measured from morning to evening, from one year to the other, time specified in the twenty minutes designated to present a speech, time as measured by the clock. This is the sense in which Paul writes in Hebrews 11:32: "for the time would fail me to tell of Gedeon, and of Barak, and of Samson."

The other Greek word for time was *kairos*. This is time that comes with unique opportunities. Kairos time exists within chronos time. It is in the sense of kairos time that the Greek philosophers would say that time was dynamic, and that nobody puts a foot into the same stream twice, for the next time one puts the foot into the stream, it will not be into the same flowing body of water.

Chronos time returns, but the kairos does not. Mondays will always come, and Christmas will always come as long as the world remains, but the missed opportunities (kairos) of last Monday (chronos) may not return with another Monday. It is in this sense that Jesus says in John 7:8: "My time is not yet full come." The same Greek word is found in 2 Corinthians 6:2: "In a time accepted, and in the day of salvation have I succoured thee: behold, now is the accepted time; behold, now is the day of salvation."

THE SECOND CHANCE

Second chances do come, but they do not always come with the same opportunities or grace. As has been said, "no one makes a first impression with a second chance." The marred clay in the hands of the Potter may be redesigned into "another vessel, as seemed good to the potter" (Jer. 18:4). But what if the clay is no longer in the Potter's hand, having fled elsewhere, like Cain, of whom it was said that he "went out from the presence of the Lord"? (Gen. 4:16). Or what about King Saul, of whom it was said, "the Spirit of the Lord departed from Saul, and an evil spirit from the Lord troubled him"? (1 Sam. 16:14).

In First Samuel 15, King Saul was being given a second chance, in spite of his blunder and consequent dismissal from the throne earlier in First Samuel 13:13. Unfortunately, Saul did not recognize the chance when it came again in the form of the divine summons that he should march out against the Amalekites and wipe them out. The marching orders against Amalek carried a clause in which was encoded that second chance, a clause that hinted at his call and the anointing that had made him king, as if he had not been rejected already from that office. Technically speaking, if Saul had been rejected as king in chapter 13, on what basis was he being sent on that mission in chapter 15, and why in his capacity *as king*? "Samuel also said unto Saul, The Lord sent me to anoint thee to be king over His people, over Israel: now therefore hearken thou unto the voice of the words of the Lord" (1 Sam. 15:1).

It was as if God was saying to him, "In spite of your previous failure, I still recognize you as king, and I'm offering you another chance. You missed the first chance, which had been tied to your military confrontation with the Philistines. Here is another chance, tied to another military confrontation—with the Amalekites." Unfortunately, Saul wasted this chance as well, and as usual he put the blame on others.

There is never a guarantee that you can waste your first day and triumph in your second chance. Samson also had a second chance to square up with the Philistines who had used Delilah his consort to deceive and trick him, but this time he had to do so without his sight. Samson prayed that God would help him to take revenge on the Philistines. God gave him a second chance, but this time his life was destroyed as well when he pulled the columns down on himself and all those around him. Thank God, though, that his name appears on the list in the Hall of Heroes of Faith in Hebrews 11.

The word of the Lord came unto the prophet Jonah a *"second time,"* after he had wasted the first call. His journey, however, was not in the first class cabin of a five-star ship. He might have traveled that way if he had not lingered and missed his first opportunity. Jonah's second chance came in the form of a dreary, dingy submarine—the belly of a fish. When Jonah eventually arrived at Nineveh, there were no hotel accommodations for him, whether five star or no star. He had to build himself a survival hut, which failed to stand up in the intense heat. He had a second chance, but not with the privileges of the first.

Do not waste your day because you are banking on a second chance. It may never come for you. But if you missed a chance in the days of ignorance, then this scripture may be speaking to you, "And the times of this ignorance God winked at; but now commandeth all men every where to repent" (Acts 17:30).

CONCLUSION

The day of which we speak is a day of many paradoxes:

1. It is a day of great temptation as well as a day of great triumph, as seen in the life of Joseph.

2. It is a day of deposal and fresh appointments, as King Saul was deposed and David was appointed.

3. It is a day of divine replacements, as David replaced Saul on the perpetual throne of Israel, and Reuben, the first son of Israel, lost the scepter to Judah, his younger brother.

4. It is a day when we are not to do the right things at the wrong time or the wrong things at the right time, as we find in the life of Esau who lost everything one day by doing something he had done many times before—dining at his brother's table.

5. It is a day of fortune reversals, as seen in the life of Esther, on whose day the tables turned, causing Haman's plot to kill the Jews to come down on his own head.

6. It is a day of eternal destiny; a day that holds the double-edged sword that may cut in either direction.

7. It is a day that may pass away without fireworks, but may leave an eternal trail of pain and irredeemable sorrow. Tomorrow will always come, as long as Jesus tarries, but tomorrow does not come for everyone.

When He got near and saw the town, He was overcome with weeping for it, Saying, If you, even you, had knowledge today, of the things which give peace! but you are not able to see them. For the time will come when your attackers will put a wall round you, and come all round you and keep you in on every side, And will make you level with the earth, and your children with you; and there will not be one stone resting on another in you, because you did not see that it was your day of mercy (Luke 19:41-44 BBE).

There is a day in every person's life that never comes twice. To miss that day is to miss destiny. Unfortunately, that day doesn't ring a bell to announce its entry, and it doesn't give us time to prepare ourselves. Still, it is the day we must not miss.

A Prayer

Dear God, please grant me discernment from day to day that my *day* may not pass me by. And for what I may have lost already, oh God, please pardon my ignorance and renew my days. Help me to be ready, even if that *day* is *today*. Like David, I do earnestly pray, "O Lord my God, Teach me to number my days, that I may apply my heart unto wisdom." In Jesus' name, amen. (See Psalm 90:12.)

CHAPTER 7

The Last Chapter

When they were escaped, then they knew that the island was called Melita. And the barbarous people shewed us no little kindness: for they kindled a fire, and received us every one, because of the present rain, and because of the cold. And when Paul had gathered a bundle of sticks, and laid them on the fire, there came a viper out of the heat, and fastened on his hand. And when the barbarians saw the venomous beast hang on his hand, they said among themselves, No doubt this man is a murderer, whom, though he hath escaped the sea, yet vengeance suffereth not to live. And he shook off the beast into the fire, and felt no harm. Howbeit they looked when he should have swollen, or fallen down dead suddenly: but after they had looked a great while, and saw no harm come to him, they changed their minds, and said that he was a god. In the same quarters were possessions of the chief man of the island, whose name was Publius; who received us, and lodged us three days courteously. And it came to pass, that the father of Publius lay sick of a fever and bloody flux; to whom Paul entered in, and prayed, and laid his hands on him, and healed him. So when this was done, others also, which had diseases in the island, came, and were healed: Who also honoured us with many honours; and when we departed, they laded us with such things as were necessary (Acts 28:1-10).

The book of Acts is a remarkable book—a celebration of the triumph of the Church over the forces of the devil, and the conquest of the world by the power of the Gospel. But satan meant to write the last chapter of that book. Accordingly, he plotted against the apostle Paul, captain of the small but triumphant band of Christians. He planned death and defeat as the final fate of the man who had given life to others and led the Church in triumph. Satan plotted an inglorious termination of the glorious course of Paul and the Church.

If satan had had his way, we would have read in the final chapter of that remarkable book that the man who raised the dead was himself killed by a viper. We would have had to mourn again in the New Testament as for King Saul in the Old Testament, "The beauty of the Church slain in a strange island! How art the mighty fallen, and the weapons of war perished in the midst of the battle! Tell it not in Gath; publish it not in the streets of New York, lest the enemies rejoice, lest the daughters of the uncircumcised triumph." (See 2 Samuel 1:17-27.) But, thankfully that was all averted by the mighty power of the everlasting God.

For many people, especially true servants of God, satan seeks to do the same. He seeks to write the last chapter of their lives, a chapter of shameful episodes meant to discredit them in their final hours. Therefore, he seems not to bother much at the early chapters of their lives. Instead he hides a viper inside a bundle of sticks for the last scene of the last act—to destroy them in the last chapter of their lives. Satan knows that just one disgraceful episode in the last chapter is enough to erase all the wonderful adventures of the earlier twenty-seven chapters.

Satan could hide his viper as you go about your daily routine, your daily ministerial tasks, your job, your household chores, or your other simple activities.

For some, satan has hidden the vipers of seducers, filthy lucre, Jezebels, and Balaams. For others, he chooses the vipers of arrogance, pride, and strife. Many have fallen that way to rise no more. Satan wrote their final chapter. There is the minister once used mightily of God who died a drunkard, bitten by the viper of alcohol. There is the man who took the Gospel to foreign lands but was later caught in immorality, bitten by the viper of fornication. There is the woman who was a jewel in God's hands but fell to the lusts of the world, bitten by the viper of greed. What a bad way to end a good book! What an inglorious termination of a glorious cause!

I pray that satan will not write the final chapter of your life. May God give you discernment when the viper appears and may you instantly understand how to deal with it.

Satan's Select Audience

For the showdown satan plotted against the man of God, he assembled a select audience. He brought together Paul's captors (the soldiers), other prisoners like him, and the barbarians of the island of Melita. In the previous chapter, Paul had preached to both of the first two groups. What a select audience of enemies, "church members," and strangers, before which to disgrace Paul!

It is amazing sometimes to consider the kinds of places and people before whom satan seeks to disgrace those who have worried his kingdom. He is a schemer. He plotted to have Samson disgraced before the same Philistines God had used him to humiliate. Samson had recently shamed and plucked off the gates of the city of Gaza like chicken feathers. After Samson lost his belt and his eyes during the unfortunate heavyweight contest in Delilah's brothel rings, his captors paraded him in disgrace first through the streets of Gaza. The same devil laid a terminal snare for Moses in the course of his routine duties before the same people he had so courageously led out of Egypt. "They angered him also at the waters of strife, so that it went ill with Moses for their sakes: Because they provoked his spirit, so that he spake unadvisedly with his lips" (Ps. 106:32-33).

That is how much satan struggled to smuggle a paragraph into the last chapter of Moses' book. Moses' blunder cost him the right to the Promised Land for which he had been preparing and laboring for eighty-plus years. Like a red-carded striker in a soccer match, he was only allowed to watch the rest of the match on the screen from Mount Nebo's dressing room. (See Deuteronomy 34:1-5.)

Why did Satan choose an audience like this before which to execute his proposed plot against the apostle Paul? Those watching Paul succumb to the viper's bite would have wasted no time concluding that Paul was certainly a bad person, a murderer. That was exactly the kind of testimony satan wanted them to carry about Paul. Paul's enemies would no doubt have said, "You see, even strangers who had never met him have the same terrible opinion of him! Paul's badness needs no proving. It is so rife that every sensible person sees and smells it several islands away."

In the end, however, the audience before which satan had meant to discredit Paul was the audience before which satan fell, disgraced. He even lost the island altogether to Paul and his God. The viper lost. Paul had won the day. Everyone wanted to be associated with him, even to be prayed for by him.

Satan may assemble the worst of men so as to amplify the disgrace he intends against you. But, certainly, God knows how to turn satan's own game against him. Keep trusting.

THEY CHANGED THEIR MINDS

The news that satan gave the barbarians was, "No doubt this man is a murderer" (Acts 28:4). They believed it; they spoke it;

they waited to see their conviction confirmed. But when Paul did not fall down and die, they were disappointed.

Imagining that they had newspapers in those days, what might the early editions have said? "Saul the Murderer"; "The Hypocrite in Melita"; "Nemesis Catches Up with a Charlatan," etc. Paul would have known they were wrong but would have had little ability to defend himself. He trusted in his God and waited for his day, which would surely come.

Have you ever been unjustly accused? Have you felt the pain of false accusations and evil reports being spread about that you had no way of combating? Did you leave matters entirely in the hands of the all-knowing God?

By the evening of that day, the headlines had changed. "A Guru in Melita"; "Saint Paul the Mystic"; "God in Human Flesh"; "God Visits Melita," etc.

It does not matter how much scandal satan has spread around about you. At some point, the headlines will change in your favor. God will see to that! The lie will thrive only for a time and then it will be gobbled up by the truth, which will reign forevermore. The end will be greater than the beginning because what satan meant to turn people against you will turn them to you instead, once the lie is unveiled.

People will come seeking your help, just as they did the apostle Paul. They will also seek your God because they have seen Him deliver you. They will change their minds. The evening paper will carry a different report. The lie exposed, and the truth revealed. The bad names they had given you will change overnight. Your triumph will be proof of your righteousness, and it will establish you and furnish your new ship for the rest of the way.

MISREADING THE EVENTS

Why did everyone take Paul for a murderer? It was because a serpent fastened itself around his hand. His momentary "set back" was, for them, a sign that even God was fighting against him. Little did they know that God had brought him there as a bait to pull out the viper and destroy it in the fire, at last. They lacked a proper discernment of the situation. They misread the signs.

Almost certainly the enemy sought to use the incident to harass Paul's mind. Maybe Paul wondered, "I was saved from a shipwreck only a moment ago. Then I met a welcoming fire which seemed to me a sign of God's intervention. But now suddenly, I am facing a viper! Opposition, arrest and imprisonment, shipwreck, divine deliverance, and now a viper! Is God against me? Could the barbarians be right after all? Is it possible that they have a better discernment of the situation than I?"

Like those ignorant barbarians, there are many today who are prone to seeing every attack from the regions of lucifer as a sign of God's judgment. Your troubles, they suppose, are confirmation of their impression that you are a bad person. Don't worry about it. With time, your glorious triumph will be all the proof they need that your God is God indeed.

TAKING THE INITIATIVE

Does the fact that I know God is on my side mean that I have nothing to do myself? No. Paul stated in First Corinthians 16:9 that "a great door," an "effectual" door, had been opened before him, but that there were multiple "adversaries" to contend with before he would be able to enter through that door. If an open door did not mean passivity for Paul, it can't for you. God may be with you, but you will still have to act. Even when a door, a great door for that matter, has been opened to you, it often takes a battle rather than a folding of the hands to get through.

Paul did not wait for the viper to decide his fate. He shook off the beast into the fire. Satan won't leave you without a fight. You have to do what you can to establish your victory. "Resist the devil, and he will flee from you" (James 4:7). Shake off the beast, and he will let go of your hand and fall into the waiting fire. Do not wait for satan to act first. Stand up for yourself. Nobody rules where they have never prevailed.

DISCERNING THE BEST APPROACH

When the viper wound itself around Paul's hand, he had to decide in a split second what to do. Thank God there was a fire in front of him. He shook the beast into it. Could he have called a prayer meeting to pray against the viper? There is a time to pray, and a time to act. In this case, there wasn't time enough to call for a prayer meeting. Paul had to trust the Holy Spirit to show him the best way to deal with that deadly situation.

Paul needed instant wisdom from the Holy Spirit on the best way to approach the present challenge. He did not have to use a method he had seen others use to great success in other situations. His was a unique case that demanded its own unique approach. The "fire method" readily made itself available, so he took it. What mattered was not how the many others had dealt with their own snake attacks, but how the Holy Ghost led him in that instance. Jesus did not heal every blind man the same way. He did not raise the dead always by the same method.

"There are *diversities of operations*, but it is the same God which worketh all in all" (1 Cor. 12:6).

PAUL THE GATHERER OF WOOD

If you were the mighty and respected apostle Paul traveling with such common prisoners and in the midst of such barbarians as those of Melita, wouldn't you have considered it below your apostolic dignity to go with the other ordinary folks to gather wood for the fire? Would you have expected to be served rather than to serve? Would you have thought it the duty of all the others to serve you, the "mighty" man of God? Shouldn't Paul have considered it the place of everyone else to do him the honor of serving him? But Paul was the tent-maker who was determined not to be anyone's liability. (See 1 Corinthians 9:1-19.) He would rather serve. He did not consider himself too big to gather wood. He identified with everyone else in the cold and in the common effort to generate warmth in the present circumstances.

WHERE THERE IS FIRE

Where the fire burns, it takes less physical exertion to deal with the serpent. Often, one little viper would throw a whole congregation into pandemonium, because there is no heat there to drive out the beast, no fire in which to burn it.

What people do then, when the fire is absent, is remain at the mercy of the beast or flee in panic. Otherwise, orthodox sympathizers would resort to the more laborious method of hitting the serpent with sticks, if they could readily find them. But, where the Pentecostal fire of the Holy Spirit burns, little effort is required. We can simply shake the useless thing into the judgment fire of the Holy Ghost. Does the fire burn where you are?

THE FIRE IS AN EXPELLER

We read in Acts 28:3 that the viper came "out of the heat." In other words, the snake had been hiding among the cold, dead wood. It's the kind of place satan loves to dwell—in cold, lifeless congregations, among the dead wood (those who lack the fire of God in them). Such was the wood Paul gathered for the fire, as God shall soon gather all lukewarm persons for the fire of hell (Matthew 3:10; John 15:5-6). The heat of Paul's fire expelled and exposed the beast. Similarly, when the fire of God starts burning in your soul, satan can stand you no longer. He will run out from you, "out of the heat," fleeing for dear life.

Dead congregations are the cherished habitation of vipers— devils. Demons love to propagate that cold, or at best the luke-warm in people, so as to make God spew them out. (See Revelation 3:15-16.) Therefore, the devils will resist the fire coming into any life, because they cannot stand the heat once the fire starts. If your own fire is burning out, go gather wood for it and take time to fan the embers back to life.

I pray that God's fire will start burning in your life, in your soul, in your church; and that it will expel every viper that has been hiding among the cold dead wood there.

THE TWO-FOLD FUNCTION OF THE FIRE

The fire meant life to Paul and the others, but death to the viper. It brought warmth to the people, but judgment to the enemy. God knows what to do with the fire. Your deliverance will be your enemy's doom. God has done it many times before. The same Red Sea that opened wide to deliver the Israelites swallowed up the Egyptians. The pillar of fire that gave light to the Israelites brought darkness to the Egyptians. (See Exodus 14:19-25.) The night of lamentation in Egypt was Passover in Goshen. Lamentation arose in one part of Egypt, while celebration began in the other. The den of lions through which Daniel passed into promotion spelled death for his enemies. The fiery furnace with an air-conditioned core that protected Shadrach, Meshach, and Abednego burned hot with thermal radiation, dooming the strong executioners of Babylon even as they approached. Thank God for His great wisdom. That which is life to you will kill your enemy. Fire is not altogether judgment. It is also life and warmth. It is judgment only to the vipers and to the agents of the enemy. Your blessing and promotion will destroy your enemies.

GOD'S FOREKNOWLEDGE AND PREPARATION FOR YOUR DELIVERANCE

God prepared in advance for the serpent by starting a fire even before the viper showed up. God knows satan's next move. He will never be taken by surprise. Just as the enemy plotted against Paul and sought to write a disgraceful conclusion to the last chapter of his life, so God knew and had prepared a plan for Paul to triumph over the situation. Do not bother about satan's plots *against* you. Rejoice in the Lord's plans *for* you. He says that His plans are "thoughts of peace and not of evil, to give you an expected end" (Jer. 29:11). Satan may plan an *unexpected end* against you, but God says He'll give you an *expected end*, contrary to the enemy's plans.

If satan knew all this, he would not have dared to harass you in the first place. All the better. Otherwise the fire would have burned in vain, with no foolish viper to be judged in it. Thank God that satan is not omniscient. He does not know everything. God reads satan's moves, but satan cannot read God's mind. No need to worry then, for God is the One in control, not the devil. God has started a fire in which to destroy satan's wily schemes. Do not bother about the enemy. Focus all your attention on God. Do not worry about the enemy's plots against your future, for your future is in God's hands. God has started a fire to take effective care of satan. Thank God, He plans your deliverance in advance of the devil's attack.

DEALING WITH THE STRONGMEN

The viper is a very poisonous snake. Our text speaks of it as a "venomous beast" (Acts 28:4). No wonder when it challenged

Paul, the barbarian spectators of Melita expected the worst to happen to him. That brings to mind the lofty impressions that the army of Israel had of Goliath until God sent a *boy* to publicly disgrace that champion giant of satan. The Israelites said, "Have you seen this man? To avoid disgrace, some Israelite will have to step up. He has impeccable credentials as a warrior. He has been a man of war from childhood. He's never lost a battle. He tears his enemies into pieces with his bare hands. Nobody challenges him. David shouldn't even think about it; he's only a boy." (See 1 Samuel 17:33.)

How they contradicted themselves! They said that David could not stand against Goliath because he was only a youth, whereas Goliath, they said, had been a *man of war* from his *youth*. Is anyone ever born a man? Does anyone become a man before being a youth? If Goliath could win victories from his youth, why couldn't David also start winning victories from his youth? The fact was they were afraid and thought more of Goliath the *problem* than they did of David the *solution*.

In the same way, the barbarians had a big opinion of the viper and a very small opinion of Paul. They waited to see Paul swell up and fall down dead. Instead, it was the viper that was thrown into the fire, defeated. They were surprised. It had never happened before. They had never known the viper to be so easily defeated. They were too familiar with the record of the viper's brutalities to think anything of Paul. The other day, the viper bit King XYZ, and he fell down dead. Before that, it had spat on Lady B, and she swelled up and died. Only recently, the viper struck the governor of the city with its tail, and that man did not survive. The viper had become a known terror—the undisputed luciferian champion of the island. Its name suited it properly and struck terror in the hearts of people. It was a venomous beast, poisonous and ruthless.

Satan may have venomous beasts, but God also has dangerous men. Satan's previous record cannot intimidate us. What havoc he has wreaked in your family before now is no guarantee that he will be able to do the same thing to you. Maybe he smote your great-grandfather with his poison. Your grandfather also suffered the same affliction and your father as well. Now you think you feel symptoms of his venom working in you and you're afraid!

Don't panic and become a victim through fear. You are not just somebody. You are God's child and His ambassador. The viper may have overcome the governor of the city who knew not God, but his venom is powerless against you because you do know God. Some lady may have fallen prey to the viper's venomous bite, but that doesn't mean you will, too. You are a Child of God, washed in the blood of the risen Savior, bought with a price. You are a king and priest of God, an ambassador of the Most High. Your case is different. Fear not!

Satan may have venomous beasts, but God also has dangerous men. They say in popular Nigerian pidgin English, "Man pass man." We can also say, "trouble pass trouble," and "power pass power." In Paul, satan met his match. In Paul, the unbroken record of the viper's atrocities was shattered. After Paul defeated the viper, the islanders had nothing more to say about the swelling and death it had once inflicted. Instead, they talked about Paul and his God. Their confessions changed. The viper had been dethroned. The best in satan's arsenal had been publicly and shamefully destroyed. A new Government—that of Jesus the King—had come to power in Melita. But that wonderful Government of God could not have been established in Melita until the satanic strongman over that island had been confronted and defeated.

> *When a strong man armed keepeth his palace, his goods are in peace: But when a stronger than he shall come upon him, and overcome him, he taketh from him all his armour wherein he trusted, and divideth his spoils* (Luke 11:21-22).

That same Lord is your God. The situation you face may have destroyed many others before you, but it does not have to destroy you, for your God is an awesome God.

When the "strong man" of Satan was destroyed, the island was very easily set free, captured for God, and brought into the "glorious liberty" of the Lord (see Romans 8:21). The "goods" of the strongman were thereafter more easily spoiled. That strongman, the viper, represented the satanic force that had all those years held the islanders and the island itself in bondage and hindered their progress. But God, through Paul, set Melita free from that satanic agent. Your land can be delivered as well. It's possible that all it would take is a single bold encounter.

THE VIPER-BONDAGE

The viper represented death, opposition, challenge, and everything that satan stood for. It especially represented bondage. For instance, think about where the viper fastened itself. It was Paul's hand. Why the hand? That was what Paul used to carry out his work. It was the hand he laid on the sick for their healing. That hand represented Paul's ministry and effectiveness. The viper chose to fasten itself on his hand so as to bring Paul into bondage. The viper hoped to make his hand of little use to him. How could he lay such a viper-infested hand of bondage on anyone? Who would let him? Who wants to receive the spirit or venom of a viper through the laying on of such a hand? People are seeking to be delivered from the troubles they already have. No one is interested in increasing their troubles in the name of looking for a solution. Therefore, Paul's ministry could have been complicated and jeopardized, had the viper succeeded.

For you, your strength (or your hand) might be your business. Your finances may mean much to you and to God's work. That's where the viper would seek to attack. Someone else's hand could be the family. Satan would bring confusion to the home so as to incapacitate (if he cannot absolutely kill) the family life. Keep your watch. Whatever angle he comes from, shake him off into the fire. There is a ready fire burning before you. There is judgment already waiting for the viper.

CONCLUSION

The story began with Paul as a prisoner. It ended with Paul as a free man. It started with Paul seeking refuge. It ended with Paul as guest of the chief of the island. It began with Paul carrying the disreputable name of a murderer, although none of them had any proof. It ended with his being proclaimed a god. Satan intended to give him a terrible reputation. He left with a glorious name. It started with a shipwreck in which all was lost. It ended with a new ship "laded with such things as were necessary" (Acts 28:10). Paul came to the island as a dishonored prisoner. He left "honoured with many honours." Not only Paul but all those who were in his company shared in the blessings that came because of him. In the same way, you shall be a blessing to your family and friends. Paul had been arrested for the Gospel's sake. Now he was being honored for the same Gospel's sake, with the added liberty to preach that same Gospel and take the whole island for God.

In this way, the Lord disappointed the enemy and boldly wrote the last chapter of Paul's life Himself.

Your destiny is in God's hand. As you let Him, He, not the viper, will decide what happens to you. May He write the last chapter of your life gloriously. "Faithful is he that calleth you, who also will do it" (1 Thess. 5:24). You will be blessed as He launches you forth on your way, to display you beyond the Potter's House of re-creative communing.

*Now unto Him that is **able to keep you from falling**, and to present you faultless before the presence of His glory with* *exceeding joy, To the only wise God our Saviour, be glory and majesty, dominion and power, both now and ever. Amen* (Jude 24-25).

MY PRAYER

Now I commend you unto "Him that is of power to stablish you according to my gospel, and the preaching of Jesus Christ, according to the revelation of the mystery, which was kept secret since the world began" (Rom. 16:25). I commend you to Him who is "able to do exceeding abundantly above all that we ask or think, according to the power that worketh in us" (Eph. 3:20). And I am confident that He will "present you holy and unblameable and unreproveable in His sight" (Col. 1:22). I pray in Jesus name, Amen.

I hope to see you some day across the river; far, far *Beyond the Potter's House!* Amen.

Contact the Author

Website: www.thepreacher.info

Email: info@thepreacher.info

Phone numbers:
+234 (0) 84 812 957 (office)
+234 (0) 803 5115 164 (mobile)
+234 (0) 803 5115 025 (mobile)

Office:
9B, Iriebe Street, D/Line, P.O. Box 10974
Port Harcourt, Nigeria

Other Books by the Author

- A Feast for the Fasting
- The Last Chapter
- Chosen for Glory
- The Morning Comes
- The Law of Attraction
- Accusations
- The Man You Must Not Miss
- The Day You Must Not Miss
- Marriage: Another Perspective
- She Talked with Angels
- When Even Fishes Went to Church
- Thy Grandmother's Faith
- A Time to Weep
- Invasion From the Past
- Gifts
- Finding Hidden Treasures

- Flying Baskets
- Ministerial Leprosy
- An Appointment with Ramoth-Gilead
- Kadesh Barnea
- Operation Ziklag
- The Mystery Cup
- Breaking Up Fallow Ground
- Spiritual Warfare
- By the Winepress
- Words on Assignment
- When Chariots Get Too Slow

Additional copies of this book and other book titles from DESTINY IMAGE™ EUROPE are available at your local bookstore.

We are adding new titles every month!

To view our complete catalog online, visit us at:
www.eurodestinyimage.com

Send a request for a catalog to:

Via Acquacorrente, 6
65123 - Pescara - ITALY
Tel. +39 085 4716623 - Fax +39 085 9431270

"Changing the world, one book at a time."

Are you an author?

Do you have a "today" God-given message?

CONTACT US

We will be happy to review your manuscript for the possibility of publication:

publisher@eurodestinyimage.com
http://www.eurodestinyimage.com/pages/AuthorsAppForm.htm